Me and My Girl

usical play

and Lyrics by L. Arthur Rose and
glas Furber

c by Noel Gay

revised by Stephen Fry

ibutions to revisions by Mike Ockrent

Samuel French — London
New York - Toronto - Hollywood

ISBN 0 573 08102 6

Please note that p.ii forms an extension of this copyright page

Printed at Bookcraft, Midsomer Norton, Somerset

ME AND MY GIRL

First presented in this version at the Leicester Haymarket Theatre by Richard Armitage for Farworlds Ltd; later transferred to the Adelphi Theatre, London, opening on 12th February 1985 with the following cast:

Bill Snibson	Robert Lindsay
Sally Smith	Emma Thompson
Maria, Duchess of Dene	Ursula Smith
Sir John Tremayne	Frank Thornton
Lady Jaqueline Carstone	Susannah Fellows
The Hon Gerald Bolingbroke	Robert Longden
Herbert Parchester	Roy Macready
Sir Jasper Tring	Geoffrey Andrews
Charles, the Butler	Richard Caldicot
Lord Battersby	Bruce Graham
Lady Battersby	Denise Hirst
Mrs Brown/Cook	Myra Sands
Bob Barking	Paul Grunert
Jim Matthews/Thomas de Hareford	Robert Cotton
Tom Crane	Michael Kirk
Mrs Worthington-Worthington	Chris Melville
Lady Brighton	Cynthia Morey
Constable	David Alder
Lord Wilmot/Simon de Hareford	Kevin A. J. Ranson
Sophia Stainsley-Asherton	Anita Pashley
Alf (Barman)/Lord French	Peter Sugden
Cockney Girl/Serving Maid	Rosemarie Ford
Serving Maid	Caroline O'Connor
Serving Maid	Susie Lee-Hayward
Housekeeper	Teresa Wellard
Telegraph Boy	Peter Martindale
Lady Damming	Marisa Campbell
Miss Miles	Frances Richardson
Adrian Hareford/Barman	Ben Heaf
Jonathan Hareford/Barman	David O'Brien

with Howard Rayner, Graeme Metcalfe, Antony Simons, Mark Hutchinson, Jenny Scott-Malden, Greg Shand

Directed by Mike Ockrent
Décor by Martin Johns
Lighting by Chris Ellis

CHARACTERS

Lord Battersby
Lady Battersby
Sir Jasper Tring
Jaquie
Charles: a butler
Gerald
Parchester
Duchess
Sir John
Bill Snibson
Sally Smith
Major Domo
Chef
Cook
Farmers
Barman
Pianist
Lord Damming
Lady Diss
Lord French
The Honourable May Miles
Mrs Worthington-Worthington
Lady Brighton
Mrs Stainsley-Asherton
Pearly King and Queen
Boy
Mrs Brown
Bob Barking
Cockney Girl
Constable

Guests, servants, cockneys

The action of the play takes place in and around Hareford Hall, Hampshire; Mayfair and Lambeth.

Time — the later 1930s

SYNOPSIS OF SCENES AND MUSICAL NUMBERS

ACT I

1 **Overture** (Instrumental)

SCENE 1   Mayfair/On the road to Hareford/Hareford Hall. A summer's
evening
2 **A Weekend At Hareford** (Guests, Jaquie, Gerald)
3 **Thinking Of No-one But Me** (Gerald, Jaquie)
4 **The Family Solicitor** (Parchester, Family)
5 **Me And My Girl** (Bill, Sally)

SCENE 2   The Kitchen
6 **An English Gentleman** (Charles, Staff)
6A **An English Gentleman (Reprise)** (Servants)

SCENE 3   The Drawing-room
7 **You Would If You Could** (Jaquie, Bill)
8 **Hold My Hand** (Bill, Sally)
8A **The Family Solicitor (Reprise)** (Parchester)
9 **Scene Change: Underscore** (Instrumental)

SCENE 4   The Hareford Arms
10 **Once You Lose Your Heart** (Sally)

SCENE 5   The Hareford Hall exterior
11 **Preparation Fugue** (Instrumental)
12 **The Lambeth Walk** (Bill, Sally, Pearly King and Queen,
Cockneys, Aristocrats)

13 **Entr'acte** (Instrumental)

ACT II

SCENE 1   The Garden of Hareford Hall
14 **The Sun Has Got His Hat On** (Gerald, Jaquie, Guests, Servants)
15 **Take It On The Chin** (Sally)
15A **Playoff** (Instrumental)

The music for *Me and My Girl* is available on hire from Samuel French Ltd

ACT I

Music 1: Overture (Instrumental)

SCENE 1

Mayfair/On the road to Hareford/Hareford Hall. A summer's evening

The CURTAIN *rises*

From a sign on a lamppost we learn that we are in Mayfair. In the road is a large open car which is made up of items of luggage; the guests are grouped in and around it. A London policeman stands nearby

Music 2: A Weekend at Hareford

Lady 1	The Season in London has started to bore
Ensemble	There's nothing to do there you've not done before
Man	The people are tiresome
Ensemble	The parties a chore
	We just couldn't stay there for one minute more.

The weekends in London have lost all their fun
Now Wimbledon's over, the Test Match is done
Now Henley has finished and Ascot has run
It's time for the country, it's time for the sun

The car starts up and the guests are en route *to Hareford. The lamppost fades into the distance, the policeman is left behind*

There isn't any doubt about
The best place we know
It's Hareford Hall in Hampshire
Where the smart people go
If the Duchess does invite you
Then you're top of the tree
Thank goodness, thank goodness,
She did write to me
She did write to me

The atmosphere will lighten
When we all take the air
And everything will brighten
When we find ourselves there

*The car arrives outside the gates to Hareford Hall. The guests dismount and
the luggage is quickly disposed of by the staff and the guests*

You'll find no-one will force you
To wake up at dawn
There's breakfast in bed and
There's lunch on the lawn

And if there are inches
You'd like to work off
There's swimming, there's croquet
There's tennis and golf
With no equivocation
We can all recommend
The noble institution of
The Hareford Weekend
It has its social equal
Nowhere else in the land
There's no other home quite so stately and grand
So stately and grand

The gates open to reveal the exterior of Hareford Hall

The atmosphere has heightened
Now we're near Hareford Hall
The younger guests are frightened
Who've not been here at all

*The doors of the Hall open and Lord and Lady Battersby, and Sir Jasper
Tring, emerge to greet their guests. Gerald looks out of an upstairs window*

But you're welcome so long as
You keep to the rules
The Duchess has never
Been partial to fools
But really so long as
You know what is done
You're happy enjoying
Your place in the sun.

(The house revolves to display the interior of Hareford Hall.) There are ancestral portraits on the walls, and a suit of armour to one side of the front entrance. The room is furnished with two long tables, set as for a grand buffet, a number of dining chairs, and an occasional table, with a vase of flowers, a newspaper and a letter rack. Decanters of whisky, brandy and other drinks are in evidence, also a box of cigarettes

The servants distribute food and drinks during the following

Jaquie and Charles are standing on the steps up to the front doors, and Gerald paces above them on the balcony.

	For a weekend at Hareford
	Is simply divine
	The people, the parties,
	The food and the wine
	There's leisure and pleasure
	For everyone
	You're happy enjoying
	Your place in the sun
Jaquie	It does seem such a pity that
	They can't find the heir
	The Family Solicitor
	Has looked everywhere
Men	It's rumoured at the moment
	That he's tearing around
Women	The Duchess demands
	That the heir shall be found
	That the heir shall be found
Gerald	Listen everybody
	For the news will soon be round
	The Family Solicitor

Parchester, the Family Solicitor, crosses the balcony in front of Gerald

	Has run the heir to ground
	There's no doubt about it
	There isn't any snag
	He's dug him out of somewhere
	He's got him in the bag
	I've seen him, I've seen him, he's here and at almost any moment ——
Ensemble	Almost any moment?
Gerald	Any blessed moment he'll appear.
Jaquie	Is he dark?

Lady 2	Is he fair?
Men	Do you think we shall care
	For the new Lord Hareford?
Lady 2	Is he short?
Jaquie	Is he tall?
Maids	Do you think we shall fall
	For the new Lord Hareford?
Men	Won't you tell us if you can
	What you know about the man.
Maids	Is he what we all expect?
Lord Battersby	Is he circumspect?
Lady 3	Is he weak?
Jaquie	Is he strong?
Charles	Does he really belong?
All	Is he all he should be?
Gerald	Well very soon we will see him.
All	Very soon we shall see.

The party spirit dissolves now and the servants start clearing away some of the plates and empty glasses

Most of the guests go, leaving one or two chatting, whilst Jaquie and Gerald are closeted together

Jaquie So. Parchester's found the heir. What do you know about him, Gerald?

Gerald Nothing at all. Except that he's alive and kicking, worse luck for me.

Jaquie He's going to be rather a rich man, isn't he?

Gerald This rather dashes our chances of scooping up the Hareford "Millions" for ourselves, doesn't it?

Jaquie Possibly.

Gerald Jaquie, what are we going to do?

Jaquie Well, you could get a job.

Gerald A what?

Jaquie You know. Work.

Gerald Work? Jaquie please! Don't be disgusting. Good lord! Me, work! Disgrace the family name? Get up before noon? Earn one's living? You must be off your chump. There must be better ways of raising money than that.

Jaquie (*holding out her engagement ring*) Well, you could try selling this.

Gerald But Jaquie — that's our engagement ring!

Jaquie Sorry darling, but I can't afford to mix business with pleasure.

Gerald You can't! You won't! You couldn't!

She hands him the ring

You have!

Jaquie We live in a commercial age, Gerald. A girl must look after herself.
  If Lord Hareford is going to get the money, then I'm going to get Lord
  Hareford.

Gerald Well dash it! You've bally well gone and broken my bally heart.

Music 3: Thinking of No-one But Me

Gerald	I once had a notion that we'd get along
	I still have the notion but maybe I'm wrong
	The female emotion will thrive on — I learn ——
	A little investment
Jaquie	— and plenty of return
	Me I'm for the top of the tree
	Just you look on and you'll see
	What's going to happen to me
	I want all that money can buy
	I'll make my limit the sky
	This is hooray and goodbye
	While I'm young and healthy
	I'll find someone wealthy
	Some rich city prize
	With rings on his fingers
Gerald	And under his eyes
Jaquie	Me — just you look up and you'll see
	Me on the top of the tree
	Thinking of no-one but me
	I'll make men so fond their pulses will stir
	And I'll be the blonde that the fellows prefer
	The past that I clung to is now on the wing
	Don't care where I'm flung to
	I'm going to have my fling
	Me — I'm for the top of the tree
	Just you look on and you'll see
Gerald	What's going to happen to me?
Jaquie	I — want all that money can buy
	I'll make my limit the sky
	This is hooray and goodbye

	While I'm young and healthy
	I'll find someone wealthy
	Some big city man ——
Gerald	Who'll cancel the contract as soon as he can!
Jaquie	Me — just you look up and you'll see
	Me on the top of the tree
	Thinking of nothing of no-one but,
	Nothing of no-one but me!

The guests exit. As they do so:

Lord Battersby enters, heading for the whisky decanter. Lady Battersby arrives and Lord Battersby is abruptly halted in his tracks. Sir Jasper enters and Parchester comes in through the front doors

Lady Battersby Frederic!
Lord Battersby Yes Clara?
Lady Battersby Not a drop.
Lord Battersby No Clara.
Lady Battersby Ah, Mr Parchester.
Parchester Good-afternoon, Lady Battersby, Lord Battersby.
Lord Battersby What's all this about an heir?
Sir Jasper Eh?
Parchester Well — I ——
Lady Battersby Who is he?
Sir Jasper Eh?
Lord Battersby Where is he?

Lord and Lady Battersby bombard Parchester with questions

Jaquie Hallo, Mummy!

The Duchess enters, followed by Charles

The others fall silent

Duchess Good-afternoon, Sir Jasper, Freddy, Clara, Mr Parchester.
Parchester Your Grace.
Duchess (*looking around*) Where is Sir John?
Gerald I passed him in the hallway, trying to recover from the shock we've all had.

The sound of barking is heard, off

Sir John enters

Sir John Get off, you flap-eared idiots! Damn those poodles of yours, Maria — they take an unhealthy interest in my ankles.

Charles exits

Everyone sits

Duchess Well, now that we're all gathered, Mr Parchester has some news which affects us all.

Sir John Yes, I've heard all about it. He's found the heir.

Parchester Now you will all be aware that the last Earl of Hareford contracted an unfortunate alliance in his youth. They soon parted and she died. There were rumours of a son however, and Lord Hareford's will had to provide for the possibility of his one day turning up. I have to tell you that it is quite certain that he has turned up. The will is insistent that the heir must be a person fit and proper to assume his position at Hareford, Otherwise he cannot inherit, but is granted a generous annuity on which to live in retirement.

Gerald Yes, yes, but how do we decide whether he is fit and proper?

Sir John Well, what's his club?

All Hear, hear.

Sir Jasper Hear.

Parchester The two executors must decide, Gerald. Her Grace and Sir John.

Sir John Well, wheel him in — let's take a look at him.

Lady Battersby Yes, let's see him.

Parchester Well, before he is introduced to you all, I should say ——

Gerald Come on, Parchester, get on with it.

Lord Battersby Rather!

Sir Jasper Eh?

Jaquie He agrees.

Lord Battersby We are all on absolute tenterhooks, aren't we, my love?

Lady Battersby Frederic.

Lord Battersby My lamb?

Lady Battersby Shut up!

Parchester But I feel I should tell you that his new lordship is not perhaps quite what ——

Sir John Damn it all, Parchester, never knew such a fellow for talking. Gerald, ring the bell.

Gerald rings the bell

Sir Jasper Eh?
Jaquie What's he called, Parchester, the new earl?
Parchester William.
Sir Jasper Eh?
Jaquie (*to Sir Jasper*) William.
Duchess William — the seventh Earl was a William.

Charles enters

Parchester Ah Charles, show the gentleman in now, please.

Charles crosses to the door

Lady Battersby Does he know yet that he is the new Lord Hareford?
Parchester No. I felt it should be broken to him gently.
Charles (*opening the door and looking out*) If you would like to come this way, sir.

Bill enters; he is wearing a check suit with a bowler hat and is smoking a cigarette

Bill Oi! Oi! Cor, stone me! How do!

The family are aghast

Sir Jasper Eh? Whaddisay?
Parchester (*bustling forward*) Welcome to Hareford, William. May I present Her Grace, the Duchess of Dene?
Bill (*grabbing the Duchess's hand and shaking it very vigorously*) Nice to meet you lady — very nice indeed.
Duchess (*withdrawing her crushed fingers*) How do you do? This is an old friend of the family, Sir John Tremayne.
Bill Wotcher cock!
Sir John My God!
Duchess (*introducing Jaquie*) My daughter, Lady Jaqueline Carstone.
Jaquie How do you do.
Bill How do you do. Very nice to meet you. Very nice indeed.
Duchess My nephew, Gerald Bolingbroke.
Gerald How do you do.
Bill How do you do. Oh, I've dropped me fag in your drink!
Gerald Ooohh! Urgh!
Duchess Lord and Lady Battersby.
Bill How do you do?

Lord Battersby How do you do? I expect you'd like a drink.

Bill Rather. (*He takes the decanter from Lord Battersby and feigns dropping it*)

Lord Battersby Do be careful! That decanter is over two hundred years old.

Bill That's a stroke of luck — it could have been a new one.

Lady Battersby Frederic!

Lord Battersby Oh right-o. (*To Bill*) P'raps later, eh?

Bill (*giving Lady Battersby a playful pat on the rear*) That's right, darlin', you tell 'im. Bit of a lad, is he?

Lady Battersby How dare you!

Duchess Mr Herbert Parchester you know already — and this is Sir Jasper Tring.

Sir Jasper Whoozat?

Bill (*gesturing in bookies' tick-tack*) How do you do. Very pleased to meet you I'm sure. (*To the company*) Well, my friends call me Bill.

Parchester Shall we proceed, your Grace?

Duchess Sit down please, William.

Bill Ta, very much. (*He sits on the nearest chair and finds himself on Sir John's knee. He then tries to find another chair and finds himself sitting uncomfortably close to Jaquie. He rolls his bowler hat down his shin to rest on his foot*)

Duchess Before we tell you why you are here, we would like to know something about you, William.

Sir John Where do you live?

Bill In a distant village called London.

Jaquie Yes, but what part?

Bill All of me.

Gerald What part of London, you clot.

Bill Lambeth.

Duchess Lambeth!

Sir John My God!

Sir Jasper Lambeth, did he say?

Bill (*to Sir Jasper*) Best part of London, Squire. South of the river ——

Sir John Yes, but the thing is ... (*He crosses his leg, picking up Bill's hat on his foot as he does so. He looks surprised and returns the hat to Bill*) In a house or a flat?

Bill I've got a parlour, drawing-room, dining-room, kitchen, bedroom, bathroom. All in the same room. 'Bout the size of that fireplace over there.

They all lean forward, peering at the fireplace

The bath's in the basin. One day you bath your top part, the next day you bath your middle and the third day you bath your ——

Sir John (*hastily*) Quite, quite! What do you live on?

Bill Me wits.

Sir John You must be severely undernourished. Now look, what do you actually do?

Bill Do? Anything, Squire. I do a bit of sparring now and again ——

Sir John Sparring?

Bill Y'know; run for a bookie, sell fruit off a barrow ...

Sir Jasper Eh?

Bill Olly, olly, olly, all fresh — ripe strawberries ... And I do a bit of "quickness of the hand deceives the eye". (*He puts his hat on the table, takes a pack of cards from his pocket and fans them to Sir John*) Take a card, any card. Do I know this man? No, I do not know this man. Take a card, any card — go on ... Right, look at it, shuffle it —— (*Under cover of the cards Bill picks Sir John's pocket of his watch*)

Sir John takes a card

— but don't tell me what it is ... What is it?

Sir John Five of spades.

Bill Correct! The man wins a gold watch. (*He hands Sir John his watch back*)

Sir John Hey, that's mine. What are you doing? (*To the Duchess*) Let's just get on with it, shall we?

Duchess Now we have a surprise for you, William. Parchester.

Parchester Your Grace. Do you know anything about your parents, William?

Bill They're brown bread.

Gerald Brown bread?

Duchess What are you talking about? Brown bread?

Bill Like I said, brown bread — dead!

Gerald Oh, it's cockney rhyming slang. Oh, goody! I say, can you do that?

Sir John Rhyming slang?

Gerald (*enthusiastically*) Yes, you hear it all the time at the races ... um, apparently — so I'm told.

Parchester Well, quite. The facts are these. Your late father was the Earl of Hareford. You were his only son. Therefore, William Percival Presteigne-Snibson, you are now the rightful and lawful 18th Baron Haveringland, Lord of the Stimpson Marshes, Marshall Royal in Ordinary to the Stewardy of Brandiston with Castle Dalling and 14th Earl of Hareford.

Bill (*turning to the family*) 'ere ... (*He turns back to Parchester*) But ...

There is a silence; all eyes are on Bill. A smile slowly spreads across his face and he nudges Parchester

Gettaway! You're pulling my tinkler, encha?

Sir John Nothing could be more serious.

Bill drops to the floor in a dead faint

Good Lord, he's fainted. Quick, water.
Bill (*reviving*) 'Ere, I didn't faint for water.
Sir John Have a little brandy then. (*He proffers the decanter*)
Bill (*taking a swig from the decanter*) Brandy! That'll do, guv; thanks squire, cheers.

Bill is helped to a chair

Duchess This is your family. Your father was my brother, you may therefore refer to me as your Aunt Maria. Lady Jaqueline and Gerald are your cousins.
Bill What him? (*He points at Gerald*)

Gerald slams Bill's hat on to Bill's outstretched hand; Bill reacts in pain as if his finger has been crushed

(*To Sir John*) Hallo, Uncle John.
Sir John Uncle John?
Bill (*to the Duchess*) Ain't you two married then?
Duchess Certainly not!
Bill Oops, naughty naughty. So this is my family? Me — an Earl — the Earl of Hareford? (*A thought strikes him*) 'Ere, am I rich then?
Parchester Well, now you have about a hundred thousand pounds
Bill Yeah, that's not bad, is it .. ?
Parchester A year ...
Bill I think I'm going to faint again. I said I think I'm going to faint again.
Lord Battersby Oh rather. (*He gives Bill the decanter*) Cheers.
Sir Jasper Nothing wrong with Lambeth, old cousin Thomas used to live in Lambeth.
Lady Battersby Of course he did, Sir Jasper, he was the Archbishop of Canterbury.
Bill One hundred thousand crispies a year, cor dear oh dear! Well, I'll take this year's instalment and leave you good people be, then.
Parchester Ah, I'm afraid it's not quite as simple as that.
Duchess You are not allowed to touch the inheritance ——
Bill The how much?
Duchess The money, unless the executors of your father's will, that is Sir John here and myself, are agreed that you are a fit and proper person to stay on here as master of Hareford. Otherwise you will receive an annuity and live in retirement.

Bill Fit and proper? Me? For you lot? Forget it.

Sir John Quite right. Sensible attitude.

Duchess Nonsense. You are Lord Hareford. As Lord Hareford you will stay at Hareford.

Sir John Maria, what are you saying? The man's an outsider, pay him off.

All Quite right. He's impossible. (*Etc.*)

Duchess I will educate you. I am confident you will learn to rule Hareford. If you do as I bid you, blood will tell.

Sir John If you don't, blood will flow.

Duchess You are the last of the line. It is your duty to stay here and perpetuate the family.

Bill Perpetuate. Strewth! You wait till I show all this to Sally.

Jaquie Sally?

Bill Yeah, she's my girl. She's gonna love all this ...

Duchess This — Sally, is she also from ——

Bill Lambeth? Yeah, 'course.

Duchess Lambeth.

Sir John My God!

Parchester I should perhaps have mentioned, William, that it is a condition of the will that you marry a fit and proper consort.

Bill Sally's fit for me all right. She comes with me in the car. I'll get her in. (*He puts his fingers in his mouth and emits a piercing whistle*)

Sir John Don't do that!

Bill All right, calm down. I'll go and fetch her in. (*He heads for the door, handing Sir John his watch again as he passes*) Keep an eye on the time, mate!

Duchess Just one moment. The will states you must marry a woman of your own class.

Bill That's all right then, 'cos Sally is my own class.

Duchess Not any longer. You may bring her in and tell her who you really are, and then the car will take her back to Lambeth.

Bill (*challenging the Duchess*) Oh, yeah? We'll soon see about that, me old fruit. (*To Jasper*) Me old fruit! (*He heads for the exit, shouting off*) Oi! Sal!

He exits

Duchess Well!

Sir John Well!

Jaquie Well!

Gerald Well!

Lady Battersby We shan't have a penny!

Sir John I can just see the newspaper headlines. "Hareford's Cockney Lord, Jellied Eels on the Crown Derby!" My God, Maria, you can't let this costermonger take over Hareford.

Duchess The family needs new blood.
Sir John You call that new blood? Hang it all Maria, what are we going to
do?
Duchess Mr Parchester is here to advise.
Gerald Dear Mr Parchester. Please do advise.

Music 4: The Family Solicitor

Parchester	As the Family Solicitor
	Here's my advice to you
	As the Family Solicitor
	Here's what you ought to do
	For six and eight I'll put you straight
	If anything goes wrong
	For I contend you must pretend
	That life is one sweet song
	So sing a little and dance a little
	Be gay a little and play a little
	Bring your troubles more and more
	To the Family Solicitor
	Say a little and think a little
	Eat a little and drink a little
	Keep a drop of the ninety-four
	For the Family Solicitor
Duchess	He'll take all your cases
	Keep you in your places
Sir John	Maybe save your faces
Family	Ha! Ha! Ha! Ha! Ha! Ha! Ha! Ha!
	Sing a little and dance a little
	Be gay a little and play a little
	Bring your troubles more and more
	To the Family Solicitor
Parchester	Say a little and think a little
	And eat a little and drink a little
	Keep a drop of the ninety-four
	For the Family Solicitor
	He'll take all your cases
	Keep you in your places
	Maybe save your faces
	Ha! Ha! Ha! Ha!
Ladies	Ha! Ha! Ha! Ha!

Gentlemen	Ha! Ha! Ha! Ha! Ha! Ha! Ha! Ha!
Gerald	Hop a little and skip a little
Sir John	And jump a little, let rip a little
Sir Jasper	Thank your lucky stars once more
Battersby	For the Family Solicitor
Parchester	Hop a little and skip a little
	And jump a little, let rip a little
	Thank your lucky stars once more
	For the Family Solicitor
Family	Hop a little and skip a little
	And jump a little, let rip a little
	Thank your lucky stars once more
Parchester	For the Family
Family	Ha! Ha! Ha! Ha! Ha! Ha! Ha! Ha!
Parchester	The Family
Family	Ha! Ha! Ha! Ha! Ha! Ha! Ha! Ha!
	For the Family Solicit——
Parchester	— tor!
Family	The Family Solicitor
	The Family Solicitor
	The Family Solicitor
Parchester	For the Family Solicitor.

Duchess (*speaking*) I shall take a walk in the rose garden to compose myself.

She exits

Gerald Thank you very much for that useless advice Parchester, but it looks like the workhouse for us.

Sir John That man has to go. I want him out of the house. Parchester, is there nothing we can do?

Parchester Well, we could examine the original will, perhaps.

Sir John For a loophole?

Parchester Yes, for a loophole.

Sir John Where is the will?

Parchester In the library.

All The library.

Sir John Then what are we waiting for?

Everyone exits apart from Sir Jasper

Sir Jasper I say, wait for me!

He exits

The front door opens and Bill pokes his head round

Bill It's all right, Sal, you can come in now, they've all gone.

Sally enters, nervously looking about her

Sally Cor! It's the bleedin' Odeon.
Bill You wouldn't get this in no Odeon. Would you care to dine with me, Miss Smith?
Sally Ooh Bill. It's bigger than the British Museum!
Bill It's cleaner and all. (*He points to the floor*) You could eat your dinner off that floor.
Sally (*holding up a newspaper from the table*) You don't have to, they've even got posh newspapers to eat your chips out of.
Bill (*holding up a decanter*) And look at the size of the vinegar bottles!
Sally Bill, I still can't believe it.
Bill It's true. I tell ya. My aunt's a Duchess, so that makes me ——
Sally Dutch?
Bill No, a Lord! I am a Lord.
Sally So this is your house?
Bill Yeah, this is my house — well, our house. I know, not very 'omely is it?
Sally Oh, I'll soon change all that when we're married. I'll clear out all this old rubbish — and that old iron. (*Referring to the suit of armour*)
Bill Bung up a nice bit of flowered wallpaper, or something.
Sally Yeah! Shove in some *new* furniture, net curtains, bit of lino — oh Bill, we'll have a lovely motor-car.
Bill Not 'alf. You'll be my — what's an earl's wife called?
Sally An earless?
Bill Yeah, you'll be my earless.
Sally Bill, when I'm an earless I won't have to work down the fish market no more. I'll be able to have a little dress shop! I've always wanted a dress shop.
Bill Leave it out, girl, you won't need to work.
Sally Oh, I'll be able to have me 'air permed.
Bill And you'll have your fingers manacled.
Sally And me toes chiropodized. And you'll buy me lots of scent.
Bill Course I will. We'll get rid of that fish smell somehow, girl.
Sally And when I smell luscious we can sit in the pictures in the three and sixpennies 'stead of the one and threepennies.
Bill Coo, it's a dream, innit?

They kiss

(*After a beat*) 'Ere, I gotta be ejercated.

Sally Ejercated? Who says?

Bill The executors. That's my aunt and Sir John.

Sally Are they the executors?

Bill Yeah, not 'alf! They chop off the dough if I don't come up to scratch.
I got a lot to learn, girl. Work fast, do a lot of perpetuating.

Sally (*as this sinks in*) Oh yeah? And where do I fit in?

Bill What d'you mean?

Sally Am I going to be staying here as well?

Bill Well, we'll sort something out. She's a bit of a dragon is that Duchess.
P'raps there's a pub nearby, you could stay there for a few nights.

Sally Bill, all this ain't going to part us is it?

Bill Leave it out! Nothing's going to part me and my girl.

Sally If they make you marry one of *their* lot, I'd *die* an old maid.

Bill And so would I. Hey, Sally, I couldn't live without you.

Sally And I couldn't live without you, Bill.

Bill You're all I've got.

Music 5: Me and My Girl

Bill   Life's an empty thing
                     Life can be so awful lonesome
                     If you're always on your ownsome
                     Life's an empty thing

Sally   Life's a different thing
                     When you've found your one and only
                     Then you feel no longer lonely
                     Life's a happy thing

Bill   Everything was topsy-turvy
                     Life seemed all wrong
                     But it came all right as soon as
                     You came along

                     Me and my girl, meant for each other
                     Sent for each other, and liking it so
                     Me and my girl, 's' no use pretending
                     We knew the ending a long time ago

                     Some little church, with a big steeple
                     Just a few people that both of us know
                     And we'll have love, laughter
                     Be happy ever after, me and my girl.

Sally   I love to hear you saying ——
                     Me and my girl, meant for each other
                     Sent for each other, and liking it so
                     Me and my girl, 's' no use pretending
                     We knew the ending a long time ago
Both   Some little church, with a big steeple
                     Just a few people that both of us know
                     And we'll have love, laughter
                     Be happy ever after, me and my girl

Dance; they end up sitting on the table

                     And we'll have love, laughter
                     Be happy every after, me and my girl.

They kiss and fall backwards off the table

Charles enters with footmen. He crosses to the table and raises the tablecloth, revealing Bill and Sally beneath

Charles Good-afternoon, my Lord.
Bill Er, wotcher cock, all right?
Sally (*indicating the footmen*) Are they waxworks?
Bill No, they're usherettes.
Sally It is the bleeding Odeon.
Charles May I, on behalf of the staff, welcome you to Hareford, my Lord.
Sally Lumme. He called you "my Lord".
Bill I know. Thank you very much, cheers, guv. This is Sally.
Sally Pleased to meet you. I'm sure. Ever so.
Charles Aperitif, my Lord?
Bill Eh?
Charles Aperitif, my Lord?
Bill No thanks, I've got my own.
Charles A glass of wine, Miss?
Sally Thanks a bunch.
Bill You haven't got a fag 'ave you, mate?
Charles Certainly, my Lord.

Charles opens a cigarette box and offers it to Bill. A footman pours two glasses of wine

Bill Cheers, squire. Can Sally have one an' all?
Charles They are all yours, my Lord.

Bill Eh?

Charles Everything here is the property of your Lordship.

Bill Ooh Sal — take the whole boxful. (*He takes a handful of cigarettes and gives them to Sally*)

Sally Bill.

Bill Take the bleedin' box then. (*He gives the box to Sally*)

Sally (*putting the box into her pocket*) Bill!

Bill Well, it's all mine now, innit? 'Ere are, what about something for your lodgings in Lambeth? Oi! A cumfy chair.

Bill picks up a chair and hands it to a footman

Bung it in the Riley, Smiley.

The footman takes the chair off

(*Pointing to a letter rack*) Bill, could I have that, 'cause I've always wanted a toast-rack?

Bill 'Course you can. (*He gestures to Charles*) Bung it in the Morris, Horace. (*He takes a sword from the suit of armour*) You'll need this in case anyone tries to rob you.

He gives the sword to another footman

Bung that in the Ford, Claude.

Sally And I think I'll take the rest of it for our honeymoon.

Bill Are you sure this is mine?

Charles Everything here is your Lordship's property.

Bill Don't argue with the man, Sal. Just take the bleedin' lot!

Sally Right!

Bill and Sally pick up the silver from the table

Charles Would you care for a box, my Lord?

Bill A box! Don't be daft! I've got enough to carry as it is!

The Lights fade; the set transforms into the kitchen

Need kitchen staff.

SCENE 2

Front of tabs.

The Kitchen

UL, *by the entrance, various pots and pans are boiling away on the kitchen range.* UR *stands the kitchen sink by the dumb waiter. The two buffet tables*

*from the previous set have been stripped of their cloths, and are now plain
deal tables*

*The Lights come up. The staff and servants are gathered in the kitchen, where
Charles directs them in the preparation of a meal for the Hareford family*

Music 6: An English Gentleman

Charles ⎫	William of Hareford is diametrically
Staff ⎭	In reality, theoretically
	Quite opposed, and that pathetically
	To all that appertains to gentle folk

So we face with great dubiety
This sad lack of pure propriety
He's no sense of High Society
The fellow even calls himself a bloke

Charles	He takes his food with a horrid zest
	He eats one half and he wears the rest
Maids	Though it may be true that his blood is blue

*The Chef whispers the next line to the parlour maid, who drops the plate she
is holding*

Chef	It is nothing like as purple as his language
All	He's rough! He's crude! He's tough! He's rude!
	By all of us it's understood
	He'll never make the noble rake
	That constitutes a gentleman, an English gentleman.

The bell rings

Charles and the upstairs staff exit briefly, then return

Major Domo ⎫	We served him peas and they all shot forth
Footman 1 ⎭	
Maid 1	To the East
Maid 2	And West
Maid 1	To the South
Maid 2	And North
Major Domo	Then he let one fly and it struck the eye of Lady Margaret
	Leicester!
All	Poor Lady M, what a fearful bore

She's never had a pea in her eye before
He's rough! He's crude! He's tough! He's rough!
Bill voice (*via speaking tube*) More bleeding chutney!
All   He's rude
By all of us it's understood
He'll never make the noble rake
That constitutes a gentleman, an English
Gentleman, an English gentleman,
That constitutes a gentleman, an English gentleman.

Bill enters wearing riding gear and walking bow-legged

Bill Oi! Oi! Give us beer, Charlie.
Charles Pleasant ride, my Lord?
Bill Pleasant ride? I'm going to have to put that horse on a diet. It'll take me a week to straighten these legs.

Charles hands him his beer

Thankee, Oats.
Charles Oats, my Lord?
Bill Oats. Oats and Barley — Charlie.
Charles Her Grace does not wish you to call me anything but Charles, my Lord.
Bill You should hear what I call her sometimes.

The Cook passes, stirring a saucepan

Bill Oh my Gawd, Maude! What's that?
Cook It's bean soup.
Bill I don't care what it's been, what is it now?
Major Domo The family thinks you are too convivial with us, my Lord.
Bill Convivial — convivial! (*He pinches a maid*)

The maid thinks a footman pinched her; she slaps the footman's face

What's the matter with you lot, eh? Gor blimey! The family look down on me, and you lot look up at me. I'm 'emmed in, like the 'am in the sandwich. I think I'll go down to the old rub-a-dub-dub.
Maids Eh?
Bill The pub.
Maids Ohhhh.
Bill To see Sally.

Charles Her Grace doesn't approve of you meeting Miss Smith at the — uh — rub-a-dub-a-dub, my Lord.

The servants mutter in disapproval

Bill Well, it's my life, innit?
Charles It is indeed, my Lord, it is also your pub.
Bill Eh?
Charles The *Hareford Arms* is part of your Lordship's estate.
Bill Strewth!
Maid My Lord, Lady Jaqueline awaits your Lordship in the Rose Drawing-room.
Bill The Rose Drawing-room? Where's that?
Charles It is in the East Wing, my Lord, just south of the Morning Room, west of the Billiard Room; but if your Lordship would like a footman to guide you there ...
Bill No thanks, just give me a compass and a biscuit ration. I'll find it on me own. If Sally comes round, tell her to come and rescue me.
Chef My Lord, her Grace's maid overheard her saying she means to part you and Miss Sally.
Bill Eh?
Maid She don't like your Lordship visiting Miss Sally in the *Hareford Arms* and treating the locals there ——
Footman 1 — and playing darts and shove ha'penny with them.
Bill I dunno, King Edward never 'ad this trouble. One speech on the wireless and 'e and 'is missis were shot of the lot of them. I know just 'ow 'e felt.

Music 6A: An English Gentleman (Reprise)

Servants (*singing*)   By all of us it's understood
He'll never make the noble rake
That constitutes a gentleman, an English gentleman,
That constitutes a gentleman, an English gentleman.

The Lights fade

SCENE 3

The Drawing-room

The scene is backed by the drawing-room windows, overlooking the grounds

The footmen deliver a small chesterfield to the R, and move one of the long tables L as a desk, adding several letters and a bell

Bill walks gingerly to the sofa and sits, still with his beer

Charles takes Bill's beer and exits

Jaquie enters, unseen by Bill, and perches on the arm of the sofa

Bill rests his elbow on the arm of the sofa, and unwittingly puts his hand on Jaquie's thigh

Bill Oh my Gawd!

Jaquie Well, here we are again.

Bill (*eyeing Jaquie's limbs*) Yes. I'm seeing rather a lot of you lately.

Jaquie I thought we might meet this morning, as Mummy has suggested that I take you in hand. To teach you about art and literature and life. Are you familiar with any of our great novelists? Dickens? Thackeray? Do you like Kipling?

Bill I don't know, I've never kippled.

Jaquie Bill, you and I are soul mates, I can look deep into your eyes and see what you're thinking.

Bill Then why don't you slap my face?

Jaquie You're a man. I'm a woman.

Bill (*in astonishment*) Oh my Gawd! So you are.

Jaquie I can see it all so clearly.

Bill (*gulping*) Not as clearly as I can.

Jaquie I'm on a ship with you — sailing away. I'm abroad.

Bill You're telling me!

Jaquie Italy! Beautiful Florence. Just we two making love.

Bill What, you and Florence?

Jaquie You kiss me on the piazza.

Bill I never do!

During the following, Jaquie advances on Bill; he hastily puts cushions between himself and Jaquie, each cushion being smaller than the one before

Jaquie (*with devastating vamp*) I believe if two people are attracted to each other they should cast convention to the winds. Nothing should come between them and their destiny. It is useless to resist. Can't you feel my heart pounding? (*She takes his hand and places it on her bosom*)

Bill Oi! Oi! Oi! Don't start all that. Cor strewth! Someone might come in.

Jaquie Let them come in, Bill. Let the whole world come in. What have I got to hide?

Bill Well ... there's ...

Jaquie Oh, Bill, if only you knew how long I've been waiting for you.

Bill I was only downstairs.

Music 7: You Would If You Could

Jaquie (*singing*) How I've looked for someone who
Plays upon my heart like you
Tall and dark and handsome and sweet
Someone who would take my heart
Maybe tear my soul apart
See I lay myself at your feet

You would if you could
You could and you should
And you would if you could
Bill But I can't.
Jaquie I'm sure that you can
I know you're a man
And you would if you could
Bill But I shan't.
Jaquie When you're a bad boy
You go my way
But you're a good boy
And so you say regretfully

You would if you could
You could and you should
And you would if you could
Bill But it's impossible.
I might put my arms round you
Do the things that most men do
Men not so high-minded as I
I can't do that caveman stuff
Sock 'em hard, treat 'em rough
Mother wouldn't like me to try
Jaquie You would if you could
You could and you should
And you would if you could
Bill But I don't.
Jaquie I'm sure that you do
Just look at the view
And you would if you could
Bill But I won't
Jaquie You're like an apple on top of the tree
I'd like to shake you

I'd like to see you falling for me

Bill   I would if I could ——

Jaquie   Bill — you could and you should

And you would if you could, Bill, and I ——

Bill is about to succumb; he opens his mouth to sing "And I will", a moment taut with all the exploding eroticism of the "Liebesnacht" from Tristan and Isolde, *when :*

> *Gerald and Sally enter. Gerald is wearing cricket whites and pads and carries a cricket bat*

Bill I really think it's out of the question!

Bill overbalances and topples over the edge of the sofa. Jaquie turns round to see Sally and Gerald

Jaquie Hallo, Gerald.
Gerald Hallo, Gerald?
Jaquie I was just giving William an etiquette lesson.
Gerald Oh really? Jaquie, I'm shocked. I'm astonished. I'm amazed. You are looking at a highly disturbed person.
Jaquie Oh really, Gerald, do you mind?
Gerald Yes, I do. (*He hits one of his pads with the bat and, after a moment, recoils in pain*) I'm staggered and jiggered and profoundly startled. I am going upstairs to bathe my temples in eau de Cologne.

> *He exits*

Bill ties his white necktie to his riding crop and waves it above the sofa in a show of surrender; he then comes up from behind the sofa

Bill Oh 'allo, Sal.
Sally Bill, would you 'ave the goodness to present my compliments to Lady Jaqueline and tell her that I would like to have converse with you alone?
Jaquie William, please tell Miss Smith that I was just leaving, I detect an odour of prudishness in the air.
Sally The smell to what 'er Ladyness is referring, William, seems to come from some cheap French scent in the neighbourhood of that settee.
Jaquie Perhaps Miss Smith is not aware, William, that such gross impertinence betrays her obvious lack of breeding.
Sally Thank 'er Ladyship for me, William, and tell her that if I want lessons in her kind of breeding, I can go to a farmyard.
Jaquie How dare you!
Bill Ooh! Cock a doodle do!

Jaquie William, I'll see you later, when your little friend has gone.
Sally That's right, dear, you run off and sew up your frock.

Jaquie exits in high dudgeon

Bill Ooh! Saucer of milk for Miss Smith.
Sally She don't 'alf get my dander up, that one.
Bill Yeah, I know what you mean, girl. Still, never mind 'er, 'ow's my girl?
(He moves to her)
Sally *(repelling his advances)* I don't like coming round here, Bill. The
Duchess don't want me to.
Bill The Duchess? What's she got to do with it? I want you to, don't I? This
is my house; if you go, I go.
Sally She's right. As long as I'm around, you can't grow into a gentleman.
You'd best forget me.
Bill Forget you? Forget you? I could no more forget you than I could forget
... whatsisname.

She laughs

Music 8: Hold My Hand

Bill	You require a lot of looking after
	That's a job in which I take a pride
Sally	You can always make me smile
	Make my journey seem worthwhile
Bill	Why not keep me always at your side
	To guide you?
	Hold my hand
	No matter what the weather
	Just you hold my hand
	We'll walk through life together
Sally	For you'll find in me
	That kind of a friend
	Who will see me through to the end
Both	So if you'll hold my hand
	We both shall walk more steadily
Bill	For understand
	You hold my heart already
Sally	In that
Sally **Bill** }	Dreamland

Where I have planned
That I shall hold your hand forever

Jaquie and the dancers enter. They dress Bill for cricket, adding a cap and pads and handing him a bat

Sally runs off, followed by Bill, who is followed by Jaquie

Dance break

As the number ends the Duchess, Sir John and Parchester enter

Duchess If you're going to play, play outside.

The dancers exit

The Duchess and Sir John sit on the sofa. Parchester busies himself with letters at the desk

Sir John Maria, why are you persisting with this nonsense? Nothing you can do or say will make me believe that William could be made remotely fit or proper for Hareford.
Duchess We shall see. I have sent for him.
Sir John You and I used to understand each other.
Duchess Sir John!
Sir John Remember, when we were young. I used to climb that old cherry tree in your father's orchard. I'd throw down all the best fruit for you.
Duchess And we'd eat until we felt sick

They both laugh

Sir John We were very ... close in those days.

Two footmen enter, carrying Bill

Bill Put me down, put me down!

The footmen drop Bill

Not that hard!

During the following the footmen remove Bill's pads, cap and bat and exit

Duchess Thank for dropping in. It's time for some more lessons.

Bill But I was just going down the pub, to see Sally!

Sir John Maria ...

Duchess I hope you don't mean to thwart me, John.

Bill Go on, John. Give her a good thwarting.

Duchess You may leave us, Sir John. We have work to do.

Sir John Back to my kennel.

Bill (*presenting Sir John with his watch*) John, take this with you.

Sir John Thank you ... (*Then he realizes what Bill has done*)

Sir John exits

Duchess Parchester, time for more lessons.

Parchester Your Grace.

Bill What's today's torture, then?

Parchester I felt we should begin with your personal correspondence. You have a great deal outstanding.

Bill Fan mail! What do they all want then?

Parchester (*showing Bill a letter*) Well, this one for instance is from Celia Worthington-Worthington. She wants to know if you'll lay the foundation stone for the new hospital.

Bill Celia Worthington-Worthington? I don't even know her-know her.

Duchess The Worthington-Worthingtons are one of the oldest families in England.

Bill Then tell her I'll do it-do it! They're not older than the Harefords?

Parchester Oh no. Your family predates them by some hundred or so years.

Bill (*tearing up the letter*) Upstarts! Social climbers! Parvenus! I'll turn them down-down. (*He indicates another letter*) What's that one there?

Parchester This is a letter asking if you would help the Old Ladies' Home.

Bill Blimey, I didn't know they were still out! I know this writing. This letter is from my old mate Bob Barking. Oi! Oi! Good old Bobby! Listen to this: "Dear My Lord." That's me. "This is to thank you for your wedding present of a bracelet. My missis is very proud of it and wears it on her PTO." PTO? What's that?

Parchester moves his wrist in a page-turning gesture

Bill Oh, wrist!

Parchester No. No. PTO. It stands for "Please Turn Over".

Bill Oh, the paper. "My missis is very proud of it and wears it on her (*he turns the letter over*) wrist." (*To Parchester*) 'Ere, you're pulling my tinkler again. (*He reads*) "We have moved into a new home near the gas works. So there is always a 'orrible smell from your old pal Bob. PS. We thank you for your invitation but we cannot accept as we are not in your class any more." Marvellous, innit? You get a bit of good fortune and your mates desert you. I'm not in his class, well I'm not in your class. And I'm certainly not in her class. (*To the Duchess*) I'm no class.

Parchester Now come along, William, we must get on.

Bill What am I to do with this lot, Cedric?

Parchester Do you want my advice?

Bill Not 'alf.

Parchester Well ...

Music 8A: The Family Solicitor (Reprise)

(*Singing*)   As the Family Solicitor
             Here's my advice to you
             As the Family Solicitor ...

Duchess That'll do, Parchester. You may leave us.

Parchester Your Grace.

He exits

Bill (*ringing the bell on the desk, then answering the phone*) Sanatorium.

Duchess Sit down, William. I have come to a decision. It is time local society had a chance to meet you. Tongues have wagged for long enough. To that end I have issued invitations for a dinner party to be held in honour of your succession. Between then and now I will teach you to behave like a gentleman.

Bill How are you going to do that, Cary?

Duchess Cary?

Bill Cary, Cary Grant. Aunt.

Duchess William, for the hundredth time — please don't rhyme! Our first task is to teach you to speak like a gentleman. Poetry therefore is out of the question. Now all speech is merely a matter of imitation. I daresay you could learn to speak like, say, Gerald, if you put your mind to it.

Bill Oh, God no! (*In a fair imitation of Gerald*) Well, really, Aunt Maria. I mean, really! I'm going upstairs to bathe my temples in eau do you do.

Duchess Eau do you do?

Bill Very well, thank you. 'Ow do you do? (*He calls off to the wings*) Charles, put the Rolls in the garage — I'll butter them later.

Duchess Perhaps a little over-zealous, but not disgraceful. This is something we can work on.

Bill lies down on the sofa

However, speaking like a gentleman is one thing, behaving like one is quite another. Already you are breaking twelve major and thirty-six minor rules of conduct.

Throughout the following catalogue of vices Bill endeavours to correct each one as it is described. This causes him to break another in doing so

Here are a few simple don'ts. Don't lie down in my presence. Don't sit while I'm standing. Don't wear your hat indoors. Don't smoke without my permission. Don't have the last button of your waistcoat done up. Don't pick up cigarette ends. Don't put your hands in your pockets. Don't slouch, don't sulk ...

In utter frustration, Bill dives on to the sofa, rolls over the length of it, and finishes standing at the other end wearing his bowler

And above all don't lose your self-control. That is the essence of a gentleman. Now, most important: when you are the host for the evening, you must go out amongst your guests, the life and soul of the party. Watch me. (*She sweeps about the stage being an imaginary hostess at an imaginary party*)

Bill watches the Duchess with ever-growing amazement

Lady Camberley! How are you? May I present Lord Edenbridge? Cynthia, my dear, you're looking lovelier than ever. And what a charming dress.
Bill Oi, Oi!
Duchess Ah, there's Harry.
Bill Oooh. Oooh.
Duchess Harry, I do believe you're putting on weight!
Bill Oh, saucepot!
Duchess How are you, Harry. Have a sherry. Sherry, dear? Sherry, dear Augustus? (*She holds out an imaginary sherry glass*)
Bill (*dipping a finger in*) Very dry sherry, Harry.
Duchess Listen!
Bill (*startled*) What?
Duchess The dance band's starting up.
Bill Oh, thank God for that.
Duchess It's playing my favourite waltz.
Bill Oh, I love it. I love it ...
Duchess Now, you must dance, like that graceful couple over there. Oh, there's Lady Lind.

Bill dashes across to where the Duchess is pointing, and greets Lady Lind as though she is only a foot tall

Bill Ah, Lady Lind, hah-de-do? (*He takes her hand*)
Duchess Go on, introduce her to someone. There's Lord Sheringham over there. Call him over.

Bill whistles shrilly

No! No!
Bill (*to Lady Lind*) No! No! Lady Lind. (*He takes her imaginary hand*) May I present Lord Sheringham? (*He looks up as though Lord Sheringham is towering above them*) Lord Sheringham, this is Amarylla Lind. Amarylla is an old friend of the — Amarylla! Keep your knickers on! No dash it, Amarylla, please. You promised! (*He traps Lady Lind under his bowler on the floor, and chases it round the stage*)
Duchess William!
Bill But Amarylla is misbehaving again. Amarylla, you will leave me alone. And come here!
Duchess Thank you, William.
Bill Oh, how do you do? This is my fiancée, Sally Smith. Isn't she a topper, bishop?
Duchess William! Sally, of course, will not be invited to this party. It is vital that you make a good impression.
Bill Nark it, 'course she's coming.
Duchess Can't you see that the more you progress, the more inappropriate Sally becomes. She understands that, why can't you?
Bill What've you been saying to her?
Duchess Never mind, suffice it to say, she knows what is best for you.
Bill Whatever you do to me, you'll never part me from Sally.
Duchess We'll see about that in due course. (*She crosses the stage towards the exit*)
Bill Auntie, mind Lady Lind!
Duchess (*to Lady Lind*) Oh, I do beg your pardon ... (*She realizes she's been duped*) Oh!

Music 9: Scene Change: Underscore

The Duchess stomps off

The servants come on to clear the furniture

Charles enters with Bill's riding mac

Charles helps Bill into the mac. Firstly Bill manages to get it on back to front. Then both Charles and Bill find they are wearing an arm each. Finally, Charles discovers that he is wearing the mac

Charles shrugs and exits

A footman helps Bill into a hunting jacket and deerstalker, completing the outfit with a double-barrelled shotgun

The servants exit and the scene becomes:

SCENE 4

The Hareford Arms

We are in the snug bar, where there is a Barman, two Farmers and Sally, plus assorted locals, including a pianist seated at the upright piano

Bill Sally!
Sally Bill!
Farmers (*realizing that Bill is pointing the shotgun at them*) M'Lord!
Bill Oh! I should bally dash it. Ha, carry on. Carry on.
Sally You don't have to play the part, Bill.
Bill It's easy, once you get the hang of this. (*He waves regally to everyone*) 'Ere Sally, what do you think, there's gonna be a party at the 'all for me.
Sally (*listlessly*) That's nice.

The pianist starts to play a gentle version of "Me and My Girl" under the dialogue

Bill It's to meet all the local nibs. It'll be a lark, don't you reckon?
Sally Well, I'm not coming. It'll only make you look stupid. Anyway, I've not been invited.

Sir John enters from the side, sees Sally and Bill, and stands, out of their sight, by the piano

Bill Don't be daft, Sally. 'Course you'll come. I'm inviting you.
Sally No, Bill. I'm going back to Lambeth. Every day you grow more and more like a gentleman and I get more and more out of place.
Bill You sound like my bloomin' aunt. Don't you love me any more? If you go back to Lambeth, I'll only follow you.
Sally But ——

Bill No!

The vehemence of Bill's reply stops the piano player and brings a hush to the room. Bill waves and the farmers, with glasses in their hands, return the gesture, throwing beer over each other

(*Tucking the shotgun under his arm*) You're staying here, and that's a bally fact.

Bill turns so that both barrels of the shotgun are aiming at the farmers. They raise their hands in horror. Bill clocks this and looking for something to do with the gun, sticks it down his trousers

Bill exits, as do the farmers

Sally BILL!
Sir John (*approaching Sally*) Can I offer you a drink, Miss Smith?
Sally No thanks. Oh, it's Sir John isn't it?
Sir John I knew the Duchess was ruining the peace of the Hall but I had no idea she was ruining your life as well.

Sally nods

Well then, it's more vital than ever that we persuade the Duchess to let William leave.
Sally But I don't want him to leave.
Sir John But he's an embarrassment to the whole family.
Sally His real roots are here. He could never go back to Lambeth now. No, I've got to leave him.
Sir John But he'll follow you and bring you back. You heard him.
Sally Not if I can think of some way of showing him how unsuitable we are.
Sir John Oh Sally, you're very fond of him, aren't you?

Music 10: Once You Lose Your Heart

Sally   Once you lose your heart, once somebody takes it
                         From the place it rested in before
                         Once you lose your heart, once somebody wakes it
                         Then it isn't your heart any more

                         It's gone before you knew it could ever go that way
                         And now you must pursue it for ever and a day

Once you lose your heart, once somebody takes it
There's one thing certain from the start
You'll find for ever
You've got to follow your heart

They say a girl should never be without love
And all the joy that love alone can bring
All that I have ever learnt about love
Tells me it's a very funny thing

For when your heart is fancy free
You hope some man will choose it
But oh the spin you find you're in
The very moment that you lose it

Sir John exits

Once you lose your heart, once somebody takes it
From the place it rested in before
Once you lose your heart, once somebody wakes it
Then it isn't your heart any more

It's gone before you knew it could ever go that way
And now you must pursue it forever and a day

Once you lose your heart, once somebody takes it
There's one thing certain from the start
You've got to follow
You've got to follow your heart

The Lights fade

Sally exits

SCENE 5

The Hareford Hall exterior

The Terrace. Early evening

Music 11: Preparation Fugue

This sequence and its snatches of stylized dialogue should be rehearsed and

*treated as if it were music. It builds rather like a fugue although it is all
spoken, with musical underscoring.*

*The major elements are: the Duchess, at her window, dressing, talking to Sir
John; Jaquie, at her window, dressing, talking to Gerald; Bill, at his window,
being dressed by Charles; the servants laying the table on the terrace: and
the rest of the family and houseguests waiting for the dinner party guests to
arrive*

Bill Dressing, dressing. The upper classes, always dressing.

Sir John Maria, I want to talk.

Gerald Jaquie, I want to talk.

Barman 1 Orange and bourbon and a twist of lime.

Footman Canapés.

Maid 1 Plates.

Maid 2 Trays.

Maid 1 OK.

Lady Battersby Lord Lincoln is coming.

Lord Battersby Sir Wilfred is coming.

Barman 2 Orange and bourbon and a piece of lime.

Bill Dressing, dressing, dressing — damn! I've dropped my stud.

Barman 1 Twist of lime.

Lord Battersby A little drink I think; I think a little drink.

Lady Battersby Frederick you don't, oh no, Freddy you don't.

Lord Battersby You're cruel, Clara, you're cruel.

Sir John You're cruel to Sally and Bill.

Gerald You're cruel to me, cruel.

Sir John They're made for each other.

Gerald We're made for each other ——

Sir John ⎫
⎬ Made for each other.
Gerald ⎭

Footman Caviar.

Maid 1 Sturgeon.

Maid 2 Salmon.

Guests The Earl of Diss and Baron Gort.

Lady Brighton Lady Simnel, Lady Smigh.

Parchester Will it work? Will it work?

Sir Jasper Eh?

Bill Blinking, bothering, bally stud. Damn, dash — dashed stud.

Charles Excuse me, my Lord — your stud.

Duchess Nonsense!

Charles Excuse me, my Lord — your stud.

Duchess } Nonsense!
Jaquie }
Charles Your stud, my Lord.
Duchess } Nonsense! Nonsense!
Jaquie }
Charles Your stud.
Bill That's half my collar.
Charles Collar, my Lord.
Bill Half dollar.
Charles Collar.
Bill Oh collar, stinking collar.

A clock chimes

Guests They're late.
Gerald He'll disgrace us.
Lord Battersby Oh golly.
Jaquie He won't.
Sir John He'll say something frightful.
Gerald He'll say something rude.
Duchess He's Hareford.
Sir John He's cockney.
Guests Lovely evening.
Lady Battersby Lovely evening.
Duchess My corsage.
Servants Where are they? Where are they?
Bill I'm scared.
Gerald This is going to be hell.
Jaquie }
Charles } Don't worry.
Duchess }
Sir John }
Bill } Don't worry.
Gerald }
Jaquie We're late.
Gerald Don't leave me.
Bill Sally, don't leave me.
Duchess Let's leave.

The Duchess and Sir John leave their window and re-enter on stage

Bill Right. This is it then.
Charles This is it.

Bill Here goes.
Charles Good luck, my Lord.

Bill leaves the window

Guests begin to arrive: Lord Damming, Lady Diss, Lord French, the Honourable May Miles, Mrs Worthington-Worthington, Lady Brighton, Mrs Stainsley-Asherton and others. Servants serve them with sherry

Footman (*announcing arrivals*) Lord Damming.
Lord Damming How do you do?
Footman Lady Diss, Lord French, and the Honourable May Miles.
Lord French Where is the Earl? When can we meet him?
Lady Battersby He's coming.
Parchester He's coming.
Charles He's ready.
Gerald He's coming. He's ready.
Lady Battersby Heavens, how's he going to behave?
Parchester I hope Her Grace has told him not to eat peas off his knife.
Lady Battersby If he calls down for a pint of mild I shall scream.
Sir John He'll let us all down. He'll make the family look ridiculous.
Duchess The family is ridiculous.
Sir John You want to be laughed at?
Duchess We will be laughed at, whether I want it or not.
Sir John Have you re-orchestrated his table manners? Taught him not to shout? Shown him ——
Duchess He'll manage. Ah, he's coming!
All He's coming.
Footman The Earl of Hareford.

Bill enters. He stands in the middle of the doorway and calmly surveys the company

Bill Ah, Aunt Maria. You look abso-bally-lutely ravishing. Welcome to Hareford Hall everyone, dash it.
Duchess (*pleased*) William.
Jaquie William ...
Sir Jasper Whozat?
Duchess May I present a very dear friend of mine? This is Celia Worthington-Worthington.
Bill Ah, Mrs Worthington-Worthington, delighted — delighted. Have you had a sherry — sherry? Gosh, I do declare you've put on weight.
Mrs Worthington-Worthington I beg your pardon!

Duchess Oh William is so original. (*She kicks his shins*)
Lady Brighton Ah, there you are, Lord Hareford. I've been dying to meet
  you.
Bill Charmed, I'm sure.
Lady Brighton Lady Brighton.
Bill Oh, I know your husband. The pier.
Lady Brighton Do you know my daughter, May?
Bill No, but thanks for the tip.
Lady Brighton Do you like your new life?
Bill Oh, frightfully. Abso-bally-lutely, yes.
Lady Brighton You seem to have done very well.
Bill Well, yes, we keep trying you know.
Footman Mrs Stainsley-Asherton.
Bill Ah, deuce it, you're late. Blood will tell. Have you had a sherry?

Bill moves towards Parchester. The Duchess greets Sophia Stainsley-
Asherton, a redoubtable, formidable-looking woman

Duchess Sophia, my dear. You know Mr Parchester?

Sophia, in a fruit-laden hat, approaches Bill, mistaking him for Parchester

Sophia How do you do, Mr Parchester. Sophia Stainsley-Asherton.
Bill Take lots of water, it'll soon pass.
Sophia Now do tell me, which one is Lord Hareford? I gather he's a complete
  outsider.
Bill So he is, yes, a complete bally bally outsider.
Sophia It's the Duchess I feel sorry for.
Bill Oh yes, me too—absolutely. The fellow's a sow's ear. Hoi polloi. Never
  be pukka, never.

Sophia turns to survey the guests and Bill dips his finger in her sherry and
licks it. He then produces a straw and drains her glass. Horrified, Parchester
whips the straw out of his grasp. Bill proceeds to eat the grapes off Sophia's
hat

Sophia Maria means to part him from some frightful Brixton girl.
Bill Oi! Lambeth, do you mind.
Sophia I beg your pardon?

Sophia goes to take a sip of her sherry and finds the glass empty

Sophia Oh!

Bill } Oh!
Sophia } Oh!
Parchester Oh!

Parchester tries to hide the straw

Sophia Which is Lord Hareford?
Parchester This is Lord Hareford.
Footman Miss Sally Smith.

Sally enters in a cockney outfit

Sally Wotcher cocks! Hiya Lord 'Areford. Seeing 'ow as like you invited me, I fought I'd come. And I brought some of our royalty along with me. This is the Pearly King and Queen of Lambeth.

The Pearly King and Queen enter

And I brought some of your ol' mates along wiv me — knowin' as 'ow you'd be pleased to see 'em.

A troop of gaily clad cockneys enters

Bill stands gaping

Sally See Lord 'Areford. You wanted me to come, but now you can see me and my friends just don't fit in, so now p'raps you'll let me get back to Lambeth, where I belong.

Everyone starts talking at once

Bill Oi! 'Ere, do you mind — you're talking to my girl, Sally. She's done all this to prove she don't belong. Well, all she's done is prove that I don't belong. I'm chucking this.
Duchess William ...
Bill It's all right Aunty, I shall retire, on the annuity.
Sally No, Bill — I didn't do this for that.
Bill Oh, come on, Sal. East End is East End and West End is West End. I'm off.
Duchess Do you think I'll be beaten like this? You'll at least stay for dinner.
Bill Well ... as long as my mates can stay.
Duchess Very well. They can stay.
Bill What about it then — you want to stay?

The cockneys agree

Bill Yeah but after dinner, I'm going straight back to Lambeth.
Duchess We'll see about that.
Bill You don't understand, do you? We could no more walk the Mayfair way,
than you could walk the Lambeth way.

Music 12: The Lambeth Walk

Bill   Lambeth you've never seen
                       The skies ain't blue, the grass ain't green
                       It hasn't got the Mayfair touch
                       But that don't matter very much

                       We play a different way
                       Not like you, but a bit more gay
                       And when we have a bit of fun — oh boy!

                       Anytime you're Lambeth way
                       Any evening, any day
                       You'll find us all
                       Doing the Lambeth walk

                       Every little Lambeth gal
                       With her little Lambeth pal
                       You'll find them all
                       Doing the Lambeth Walk

                       Everything free and easy
                       Do as you darn well pleasey
                       Why don't you make your way there?
                       Go there, stay there

                       Once you get down Lambeth way
                       Every evening every day
                       You'll find yourself
                       Doing the Lambeth Walk.

Sally   Any time you're Lambeth way
                       Any evening, any day
                       You'll find us all
                       Doing the Lambeth Walk —

Bill		Oi!
Sally		Every little Lambeth gal
		With her little Lambeth pal
		You'll find them all
		Doing the Lambeth Walk. Oi!

Bill
Sally } Everything bright and breezy

Bill
Sally
Pearly King } Do as you darn well pleasey
and Queen

Bill
Sally
Pearly King
and Queen } Why don't you make your way there
Cockney
Couple

Sally   Go there —

Sally
Cockneys } Stay there

Sally
Bill } Once you get down Lambeth way
Cockneys   Every evening, every day
              You'll find yourself
              Doing the Lambeth Walk. Oi!

              Any time you're Lambeth way
              Any evening, any day
              You'll find us all
              Doing the Lambeth Walk. Oi!

              Every little Lambeth gal
              With her little Lambeth pal
              You'll find them all
              Doing the Lambeth Walk. Oi!

During the next verse the cockneys play a "spoons" accompaniment

All   Ooh — doin' the Lambeth Walk. Oi!

              Any time you're Lambeth way
              Any evening, any day
              You'll find us all
              Doing the Lambeth Walk

Every little Lambeth gal
With her little Lambeth pal
You'll find them all
Doing the Lambeth Walk. Oi!

Everything free and easy
Do as you darn well pleasey
Why don't you make your way there?

Aristocracy   Go there
Cockneys   Stay there

All   Once you get down Lambeth way
Every evening, every day
You'll find yourself
Doing the Lambeth Walk. Oi!

Any time you're Lambeth way
Any evening, any day
You'll find us all
Doing the Lambeth Walk. Oi!

Every little Lambeth gal
With her little Lambeth pal
You'll find them all
Doing the Lambeth Walk. Oi!

Everything free and easy
Do as you darn well pleasey
Why don't you make your way there?
Go there, stay there

Once you get down Lambeth way
Every evening, every day
You'll find yourself
Doing the Lambeth Walk. Oi!

Any time you're Lambeth way
Any evening, any day
You'll find us all
Doing the Lambeth Walk. Oi!

Everything free and easy
Do as you darn well pleasey

Why don't you make your way there?
Go there, stay there

Once you get down Lambeth way
Every evening, every day
You'll find yourself
Doing the Lambeth Walk. Oi!

Any time you're Lambeth way
Any evening, any day
You'll find us all
Doin' the Lambeth Walk. Oi!

The dinner gong sounds

Charles (*speaking*) Dinner is served, your Grace.
All (*singing*)   Any time you're Lambeth way
                            Any evening, any day
                            You'll find us all
                            Doing the Lambeth Walk. Oi!

Every little Lambeth gal
With her little Lambeth pal
You'll find them all
Doing the Lambeth Walk. Oi!

Everything free and easy
Do as you darn well pleasey
Why don't you make your way there?
Go there, stay there

Once you get down Lambeth way
Every evening, every day
You'll find yourself
Doing the Lambeth
Doing the Lambeth Walk. Oi! — Oi! Oi!

CURTAIN

Music 13: Entr'acte

ACT II

SCENE 1

The Garden of Hareford Hall

US *we can see the façade of the Hall. The larger part of the stage is taken up with lawn, shrubs and trees*

The CURTAIN *rises on a frieze of guests, some dressed casually, some in tennis clothes, and servants. The family is represented by Lord and Lady Battersby, Sir Jasper Tring, Jaquie and Gerald. Croquet mallets, hoops and balls are in evidence, as are tea things and trays of drinks. Parchester is also in attendance*

Music 14: The Sun Has Got His Hat On

All	The sun has got his hat on
	Hip hip hip hooray
	The sun has got his hat on
	And he's coming out today
	Now we'll all be happy
	Hip hip hip hooray
	The sun has got his hat on
	And he's coming out today
Gerald	He's been roasting peanuts
	Out in Timbuctoo
	Now he's coming back
	To do the same for you
All	So jump into your sunbath
	Hip hip hip hooray
	The sun has got his hat on
	And he's coming out today

Gerald   Joy bells are ringing
                       The song birds are singing
                       And everyone's happy and gay
                       Dull days are over
                       We'll soon be in clover
                       So pack all your troubles away

                       The sun has got his hat on
                       Hip hip hip hooray
                       The sun has got his hat on
                       And he's coming out today
All   Now we'll all be happy
                       Hip hip hip hooray
                       The sun has got his hat on
                       And he's coming out today
Gerald   All the little boys excited
                       All the little girls delighted
                       What a lot of fun for everyone
                       Sitting in the sun all day

Gerald scat sings the next verse

All   So jump into your sunbath
                       Hip hip hip hooray
                       The sun has got his hat on
                       And he's coming out today

Tap break

                       So jump into your sunbath
                       Hip hip hip hooray
                       The sun has got his hat on
                       And he's coming out
                       He's coming out
                       The sun has got his hat on
                       And he's coming out to play!

*Jaquie and Gerald resume a game of croquet. Around them the servants
serve tea and drinks to the family and guests*

Jaquie Gerald.
Gerald Yes.
Jaquie Have you seen William at all today?

Gerald No. William!

Jaquie After last night's outrageous performance, I wanted to give him a good dressing down. I blame that upstart cockney girl. Once these types sniff money they get completely above themselves. Gerald, stand out of my way.

She hits a croquet ball into the wings, and exits, following

Gerald I say, good shot. (*He "shoots" Jaquie with his croquet mallet. To Parchester*) Herbert, where is William?

Parchester In the library. Her Grace has persuaded him that before he retires, he must at least make his maiden speech in the House of Lords.

Gerald Really! What on earth is he going to speak on?

Parchester The Public Right of Way Act of 1894. He is in the library at the moment studying the relevant dirty looks.

Gerald The what?

Parchester The dirty looks — the books.

Gerald Parchester, please, don't you start all that cockney rhyming slang. This morning he called me a daft raspberry tart. I asked him what that meant and he said it meant I was a silly nit. I mean, it doesn't even bally rhyme. Tart and nit don't rhyme.

Parchester Perhaps it's blank rhyming slang.

Gerald What?

Parchester Well. Shakespeare wrote in blank verse and everyone knows blank verse is non-rhyming verse. Well perhaps this is blank rhyming slang. You know, "Cain and Abel" — chair. "Rosie Lee" — coffee, "loaf of bread" — elbow, that sort of thing.

Gerald Do you know, he's turning the whole world stark staring mad.

Sally enters with a suitcase

(*To Sally*) The sooner he bally goes, the bally better.

Gerald exits

The Duchess and Sir John enter. They approach Sally

Charles enters from the house

Duchess Thank you for coming out, Sally, I wanted to speak to you before you return to London. You know it's quite impossible for William to go back to Lambeth with you.

Sally 'Course I do. What d'you think I was trying to show him last night?

Sir John Maria, you can't still mean to ——

Duchess Oh, do be quiet, you futile man. (*To Sally*) I appreciated what you tried to do. Unfortunately it had the opposite effect. Therefore you must go to Bill ——

Sir John Maria, it crossed my mind ——

Duchess Not a long journey. You must speak to Bill and break it off finally. Once and for all. Tell him you no longer love him.

Sally But even if I go, he'll only follow me. You heard what he said.

Duchess Oh, I think you could stop him following you, Sally. If you really wanted to. If not ...

Sally Yes, I know. Well, I won't spoil his chances. He means too much to me for that. Leave it to me.

Duchess You'll find him in the library.

Sally What's he doing there?

Duchess He's preparing his maiden speech for the House of Lords.

Sally Oh.

Duchess After you've seen him, I will give orders for a car to take you back to Lambeth. You must make sure that he has no intention of following you.

Sir John Maria, you're a wicked interfering old bat.

Duchess I'm impervious to flattery. Come, Parchester.

The Duchess exits, followed by Parchester

Sir John (*swigging a drink*) You can't let her do this to you.

Sally But she's right. Bill belongs here. I don't.

Sir John You must stand up to her. (*He sways*) Show her who's boss.

Sally She already knows who's boss. She is.

Sir John Leave it to me. I'll tell the old witch — witch.

The Duchess enters

Which reminds me, it's my shot, I think.

The Duchess and Sir John exit

Sir Jasper crosses to Sally

Sir Jasper Are you all right? Have you been crying?

Sally No, I'm all right. People often look like they're crying when really they're sort of laughing.

Sir Jasper Eh?

Sally I'm laughing.

Sir Jasper What?
Sally I'm laughing.

During the following song the scene changes to the library

Music 15: Take It On The Chin

Sally (*singing*)   Once my father said, and my mother said
And my sister said, and my brother said
Now you're growing up soon you're going to fall out
Of the family roundabout

Then my father said, and my mother said
And my sister said, and my brother said
There's one little thing you should certainly know
When into the world you go

Take your troubles on the chin
And though you get an earful
Don't despair or tear your hair
For heaven's sake keep cheerful

That's what father said, that's what mother said
That's what sister said, that's what brother said
They were certainly right in telling me so
And I think you should know

Here's a little trick
Whenever things get a little bit thick
Just you take it on the chin
Turn on a little grin
And smile, smile

Here's a little ruse
To counteract an attack of the blues
Just you take it on the chin
Turn on a little grin
And smile
Sir Jasper (*spoken*) Eh?
Sally (*singing*)   What's the use of worrying
'Bout a single blessed thing
After all is done and said
Pretty soon we'll all be dead

So as we're alive
If there's a bother you want to survive
Just you take it on the chin
Cultivate a little grin
And smile

Sir Jasper (*spoken*) Eh? What?
Sally (*singing*)   Here's a little trick
Whenever things get a little bit thick
Just you take it on the chin
Turn on a little grin
And smile, smile

Here's a little ruse
To counteract an attack of the blues
Just you take it on the chin
Turn on a little grin
And smile

What's the use of worrying
'Bout a single blessed thing
After all is done and said
Pretty soon we'll all be dead

So as we're alive
If there's a bother you want to survive
Just you take it on the chin
Cultivate a little grin
Just you take it on the chin
Cultivate a little grin
And smile, smile, smile!

The Lights fade

Music 15A: Playoff

SCENE 2

? full stage?

The Library

The library shelves range across the stage, containing many and varied
volumes. Above the shelves are hung six portraits of Hareford ancestors. To
each side of the stage there stands another book-case with a classical bust
resting on top. A great shield or armorial bearing has "Noblesse oblige"
inscribed upon it

The room is furnished with a small drinks table, and a larger round table on which are heaped a number of ancient tomes, also decanters, glasses and napkins. A set of mobile library steps stand by the centre shelves, and a tiger-skin rug is spread on the floor DC

The Lights come up to reveal Bill sitting at the table, almost swamped by a huge and ancient volume, which he is studying. He is dressed in full peer's regalia — an ermine-trimmed robe and coronet. Sally is nearby

Bill My lords and your mistresses. No that's no bleedin' good! Your lordships, your worships, your parsnips, your fish and chips ... My lords, having risen to my feet on this suspicious occasion, I would like ... (*He steps forward, and we see that his cloak is trapped under the foot of the chair. He trips on it, drops the book, and sends the coronet flying*)

Sally Bill! You all right?

Bill No, I've bent me wedding tackle, ain't I?

Sally And you've dropped your cornet.

Bill Cornet. Sally, that's a coronet.

Sally You don't half look smart, Bill.

Bill Do you reckon?

Sally Why is your get up trimmed with all that vermin?

Bill Vermin? This is ermine.

Sally (*pointing at the black flecks in the ermine*) Well, those look like vermin.

Bill Yeah, they do and all. Especially that one. Oh, blimey, Sally, it's alive, we'll get rid of that. (*He pulls at a tail on one of the flecks and a mouse appears, which he throws into the audience*)

Sally What's this book, then?

Bill That is the History of the Harefords.

Sally picks up a cut-out tree from one of the pages

Put that down, that's my family tree. It's got pictures of all my ancestors from 1066.

Sally Oh yeah, I learned all that when I was at school.

Bill Then you know who came over in 1066.

Sally 'Course. The Romans.

Bill No. The Romans came over in BBC. I'm talking about 1066 AD.

Sally After Dark?

Bill No Anno Dominoes. Does Hastings mean nothing to you?

Sally Winkles.

Bill No. I'm talking about the Battle of Hastings, when 'Arold with his 'at in 'is hand was 'it in the heye with a harrow.

Sally Oh yeah, I remember now. He put an apple on his head and said "Shoot, father, I am not afraid".

Bill Aren't you getting that confused with Robert Newton and the pear tree?

(He stands on his cloak and nearly strangles himself) The man who came over in 1066 was William ——

Sally — of Oranges ...

Bill William of Oranges!

Sally Yes, with Nell Gwynn.

Bill Oh, and I suppose William of Oranges was the son of Robert Peel.

Sally No, Bill, you're mixing him up with Robert Peel and the spider. Was he one of your ancestors?

Bill No, look, let's sort this out once and for all. *(He rolls up his cloak round his arms and points at a painting)* Now you see that geezer there. That is Rupert, the Stupid Hareford. He was killed at the Battle of Hastings.

Sally Why was he called stupid?

Bill 'Cos he wasn't actually at the battle ... You see what happened was, he was camping in the field next door and he came over to complain about the noise. Stupid, see? No, we really started with King John. *(He points to a painting, then refers to the book)* That geezer there was Simon de Hareford. He forced the king to sign the Magna Carta and so founded a strong ——

He picks up the book, assisted by Sally

—— English constitution. Then he married the King's cousin and had fourteen sons.

Sally Blimey! He must 'ave 'ad a strong constitution.

Bill 'Ere, do you know where the Magna Carta was signed?

Sally Yeah, at the bottom.

Music 15B: British Grenadiers (Instrumental)

Bill lets go of the book, and Sally, unable to hold the weight of it on her own, falls to the floor. Bill walks proudly round, making his flowing cloak billow in the air, then sits on a chair so that the cloak forms a circle around him

Lumme, ain't you grand?

Bill *(climbing the library steps and pointing to another painting)* Sal, see that geezer there? That's Richard Hareford who fought Joan of Arc.

Sally Joan of Arc, but your ancestors don't go back that far.

Bill Eh? She came after King John. You're getting your history muddled.

During the following, Sally climbs up one side of the library steps and Bill climbs down the other

Oh, no, I'm not. Everyone knows Joan of Arc was married to Noah. *(She holds Bill's cloak)*

Bill Not that ark. I'm talking about the French arc. Joan of Arc, you nerk!

Bill walks away from the steps: Sally is pulled on to the top of the steps and along

She was a beautiful maiden who rode against the English with nothing but her courage.

Sally Oh yes, she rode around on a lily-white horse through the streets of Covent Garden.

Bill Don't be so bally daft. That was Florence Nightingale. (*He sweeps round again but this time misses the chair and ends up on the floor*)

Music 15C: British Grenadiers (Instrumental)

Sally (*pointing*) Oi, Houdini. Bill, who's that geezer?

Bill That's Jonathon Hareford. He's standing beside a Spanish Galleon.

Sally Don't he look lovely. I've seen him before in *Mutiny On The Bounty*.

Bill Don't be daft, Sally, those photographs were taken long before they invented film cameras. Jonathon actually saw Sir Walter Raleigh spread out his cloak.

Sally Spread out his cloak. Whatever for?

Bill Sally, surely you remember who passed over?

Sally Yes, the Israelites.

Bill You're pretending to be more ignorant than you actually are, aren't you.

Sally What would I do that for?

Bill You're trying to put me off — like you tried last night at the party. But I'll tell you this, girl, it ain't working. I'll do this speech and then you and I arc going to get married and live on the annuity.

Sally No, Bill. I've come to say goodbye.

Bill gathers the cloak like a balloon and appears to sink into the floor as it deflates

Can't you see why the Duchess has stuffed all these ancestors into your nut? To make you feel like a gentleman and me like a worm. She's making a gentleman of you, Bill.

Bill She can't make a sow's purse out of a silk ear.

They ponder the last remark

Sally Oh, can't she? She's already got you talking like the BBC.

Bill Oh, come on.

Sally And walking like Douglas Fairbanks.

Bill Don't be so bally daft.

Sally You even swear all posh. You've got to marry someone with good blood.

Bill Well, you're not anaemic.

Sally It's not blue, though. Goodbye, Bill.

Bill Here, what's going on, girl? What's up, eh? Don't cry.

Sally I'm not.

Bill Well, don't dribble down me vermin then. (*He raises the book threateningly*) Or I'll clobber you with my ancestors.

Sally It's no good, Bill.

Bill That does it! I ain't standing here watching you crying. I'm not having it, I'm going to sort it out with her once and for all.

Sally You'll never stand up to her, Bill.

Bill (*moving to the drinks table and picking up the brandy decanter*) Oh, won't I? We'll see about that!

Sally Put that down.

Bill (*putting the decanter down*) I already have. Right, now, I'm ready for her.

Sir Jasper enters

Bill swirls his cloak round in a dramatic gesture, enveloping Sir Jasper

Sir Jasper Who put the light out?

Bill sweeps out, carrying Sir Jasper with him

Song 16: Once You Lose Your Heart (Reprise)

Sally
Once you lose your heart
Once somebody takes it
From the place it rested in before
Once you lose your heart
Once somebody wakes it
Then it isn't your heart any more

It's gone before you knew
It could ever go that way
And now you must pursue it
For ever and a day

Once you lose your heart
Once somebody takes it

> There's one thing certain from the start
> You'll find forever
> You've got to follow your heart

Charles enters

Charles The car is ready, Miss.

Sally exits, followed by Charles

The Duchess enters arguing with Bill, who brandishes a cup hilt rapier. Throughout the next speech, Bill tries without success to get a word in edgeways

Duchess Silence, silence. I will have silence. The idea is preposterous. It is absurd. You know it is absurd. *Noblesse oblige.* Sally does not arise — she simply does not arise. Presently, I shall force Sir John as the other trustee to agree — God help me — that you are a suitable person to stay here as Master of Hareford.

Bill turns an imaginary crank in the Duchess's back as if winding her up

Next, I shall marry you to Jaqueline ——

Emitting a cry of horror, Bill "stabs" himself under the arm with the rapier, and falls on to the tiger-skin rug

— she doesn't love you but she wants your title and money. Nothing wrong with that. Love. Love is for the middle classes.
Bill What about the King; he married for love?
Duchess Oh, if only I could say something. If I could find the words to speak. But no ——

The tiger-skin "attacks" Bill and he fights it off, rolling around on the floor

— there you lie and chatter — chatter — chatter. Argue — argue — argue.
Bill (*as the tiger*) Nag — nag — nag.
Duchess I can't get a word in edgeways.
Bill (*to the tiger-skin*) Now listen.
Duchess William, read that motto. (*She points to the great shield or armorial bearings on which is inscribed* "Noblesse Oblige")
Bill (*making the tiger-skin read the motto, then turn to the Duchess*) Nobbles obilge.

Duchess *Noblesse oblige.* Do you know what that means?
Bill No, and I don't want to.

Suddenly one of the ancestors in the portraits comes to life. It is Simon de Hareford

Simon Nobility has its obligations!
Bill Wh ... Wh ... did you see that? That was Simon de Hareford.

Another ancestor comes to life. It is Thomas de Hareford

Thomas There's a price to pay for land and titles.
Bill That's Thomas Hareford. In one day he burnt four hundred people.
Thomas Six hundred! At your service.

Another ancestor — Richard Hareford — comes to life

Richard Riches carry responsibility!

Now all six of the portraits come to life

Bill Me ancestors!

Song 17: Song of Hareford

Duchess	The story of Hareford handed down
	Since William the Norman wore the crown
	The story of Hareford through the ages
	Tells of honour and glory on all its pages
	Noblesse oblige
Ancestors	Noblesse oblige
Duchess	Noblesse oblige
Ancestors	Noblesse oblige
All	Noblesse oblige
Duchess	Men of Hareford — the ages tell
	Knew their duty and did it well
	Cherished the proud Hareford story
	Lived and died still adding to its glory
	Hareford stands where Hareford stood
	Thanks to men of Hareford blood
	Let it go on that way — I pray that it may ——
	To the men of Hareford today.

Portrait ancestors' tap break

The Ancestors enter through the central Library shelves. They provide a pageant of the Hareford line that stretches in costume from Norman to the Twentieth century

Ancestors   Men of Hareford, the ages tell
                  Knew their duty and did it well
                  Cherished the proud Hareford story
                  Lived and died still adding to its glory

                  Hareford stands where Hareford stood
                  Thanks to men of Hareford blood
                  Let it go on that way — we pray that it may —
                  To the men of Hareford of today

Duchess   }   Noblesse oblige/Noblesse oblige/Noblesse oblige
Ancestors   }   Men of Hareford, the ages tell
                    Knew their duty and did it well
                    Cherished the proud Hareford story
                    Lived and died still adding to its glory

                    Hareford stands where Hareford stood
                    Thanks to men of Hareford blood
                    Let it go on that way — I pray that it may —
                    To the men of Hareford of today.

Music 17A: Song of Hareford: Playoff (Instrumental)

The Ancestors return to their frames

   The Duchess exits

   Sir John enters, followed by Parchester, Charles and a parlour maid pushing a tea trolley. The parlour maid exits

Bill Oh, John, thank God it's you. You should have been here a minute ago.
Sir John Why?
Bill All my ancestors.
Sir John Yes?
Bill All tap dancing. There's Simon de Hareford giving it some of this, and
   William the Conk ... there's been a right bloody royal knees-up here .. (*He
   points to the bust on the bookcase*) Look, he's still singing!

Sir John My God, you must be as drunk as I am. It's the only way with Maria. She's like Mussolini, without the charm. You need to get very drunk to face her. Very drunk indeed.

Charles hands him a cup of tea from the trolley

Thank you, Charles. Eh! (*Realizing*) Tea! How dare you? I had an aunt once who drank tea — dead before she saw fifty. Mind you the steam roller didn't help matters. The old trout should have stuck to whisky. Stands to reason. Come on, my boy, let's get you squiffy.

Bill Eh, John! She's trying to turn me into a nobble ——

Sir John A what?

Bill A toffee-nosed Herbert like you. No offence.

Sir John None taken my dear fellow. Your very good health.

Bill (*with drunken affection*) You know something funny? When I first saw you I said to myself "That is a right berk — that is a twenty-four carat gilt-faced pile of sweepings".

Sir John (*with drunken affection*) Extraordinary. As soon as I saw you, I said to myself, "Johnny", I always call myself "Johnny" you know — well it's my name, you understand. "Johnny", I said, "this man you are looking at here is a suttergipe, a guttersnipe. This is a man I would walk ten miles in tight shoes to avoid. This is nothing but an utter, unmitigated Yahoo".

Bill (*almost in tears*) That is the most beautiful thing anyone has ever said to me. (*He hands Sir John his watch*) 'Erc you go, John.

Sir John How do you do it?

Bill Have another drink, my old china.

Sir John Ta, guv.

During the following speech, Bill empties an entire decanter into a glass on the table — but the glass remains empty

Bill Guv! Don't let the Duchess hear you saying that tosh. There won't half be a lot of trouble, John.

Noticing the empty glass, both Sir John and Bill take a long look under the table

Sir John I don't think much of yours — have one of mine. (*He pours them both a drink from another decanter*)

Bill There ain't 'alf something weird going on in this house, John. And I'll tell you that for nothing. (*He tries to reach his drink on the table. He picks up a napkin and, holding an end in one hand, and using his neck as a fulcrum, he lowers one hand to the table to pick up his drink*)

Sir John Bill, the Duchess is the key. We've got to get the Duchess to see Sally in her true light.

Parchester If I can suggest, Sir John ...

Sir John (*startled*) Oh, my God! Where did you spring from?

Parchester You must both stand up to Her Grace. You must tell her, if I may use the phrase, where to go.

Sir John With knobs on!

During the following, Bill and Sir John put an arm round Parchester's neck

Bill You on our side, Cedric?

Sir John Cedric? Is that your name? I never knew you had a name, Parchester. Cedric — ugh! Well, in this battle, my boy —— (*He sees his arm and Bill's round Parchester's neck*) Good God, you've got short arms!

Bill and Sir John, acting as Parchester's arms, adjust his tie, clean his glasses, consult his watch, and stifle a yawn

Sir John In this battle, you're either with us or — you're not with us.

Bill It's all for one and one for all.

Sir John And I'm for another drink.

Bill Yeah, me an' all.

Parchester Well then, I suppose I must be with you. We must present a united front.

Sir John Good health.

Bill So what d'yer advise then, Cedrico?

Music 17B: The Family Solicitor (Reprise)

Parchester Well ...

Parchester
Bill } (*singing*) As the Family Solici ——
Sir John

The Duchess enters

Duchess That will do. Parchester, that will do! Pay close attention. I have at last succeeded in uniting the whole family in this matter.

The rest of the family enters; as they do so, Sir John and Parchester slip quietly out

We demand that you give up Sally at all costs.

Bill You and the family demand! Well, let me tell you something. We —— (*he turns and realizes that Sir John and Parchester have evaporated*) — that is, I demand that I marry Sally or die an old maid. (*To the portraits*) Whatever you lot say — 'ere, where've they gone?

Duchess William, pull yourself together and come here.

Bill I won't come here.

Duchess (*imperiously*) Come here!

Bill (*moving to the Duchess*) Shan't! Shan't, shan't. I intend to be master of my own house.

Duchess Now listen to me.

Bill No, you listen to me. You and the family can all go to blazes.

The family chatter indignantly

Parchester surreptitiously enters

Bill Stop! And he told me to tell you so. (*He points at Parchester*)

The family chatter

Stop! And Sir John told me to tell you personally to all go to blazes, and then the fat will be in the fire. (*He picks up the book*) The history of the Harefords starts with me! (*He throws the book on the floor*) And this is what I think of past history!

Duchess How dare you! This shows how much you need a proper consort to teach you how to behave. Sally is the last person for that position. The last. Finally and positively the last!

The Duchess and family leave. Sir John enters

Sir John Bill! Bill! I've just seen Sally leaving in the car.

Bill (*after a pause; genuinely upset*) She made her do it. She's made her go back to Lambeth.

Sir John I'll get Maria back — I'll show her that it's wrong to part two lovers. I'll stand up to her. (*He falls down*)

Bill 'Ere, John. John! John!

Sir John I'm here. I was just standing up to her.

Bill I want to tell you something. You know Sally — she's my girl. I've never loved anyone else. Well, you know (*he kisses Sir John on the forehead*) except you, of course.

Sir John Well, of course.

Bill She's everything to me ...

Sir John Me too. She's a hard old battleship but I love her.

Bill Sally?

Sir John Yes. No. Maria.

Bill 'Ere, John. Why is everything spinning round. What have you been doing to this room, you rascal?

Sir John Not me, old sport. Must be something to do with those damn sun spots.

Bill No, I know what it is.

Music 18: Loves Makes The World Go Round

(*Singing*)   The world keeps on turning
                    You can't stop it turning
                    It's love makes the world go round
                    An old love, a new love
                    So long as it's true love
                    It's love makes the world go round

                    Without love nobody would sing
                    Without love no wedding bells ring

                    And though people doubt it
                    They can't live without it
                    All over the world they've found
                    That love makes the world go round

Music

Bill	It's love makes the world go round
Sir John } **Bill**	Without love nobody would sing
Sir John	Without love no wedding bells ring

Music

Ancestors	Mmm, Mmm, Mmm
	It's love makes the world go round
	Ah ... Ah ...
	It's love makes the world go round
	Ah ... Ah ...
	It's love makes the world go round
Sir John	Without love nobody would sing
Sir John } **Bill**	Without love no wedding bells ring

Ancestors   Ding Dong
Both   And though people doubt it
                       They can't live without it
                       All over the world they've found
                       That love makes the world go round
                       And round and round and round and round and round
                       And round and round and round and round

Bill produces Sir John's watch and the Lights fade

SCENE 3

Capstan Street, Lambeth

A street in Lambeth with a house, No 21,with a dustbin outside, and a pub

Music 19: Lambeth Underscore

A telegraph boy rides his bike to the door of No 21, dismounts and knocks

Mrs Brown *(through the upstairs window)* Yes?
Boy Telegram for Miss Sally Smith.
Mrs Brown OK little boy.
Boy Any reply?
Mrs Brown She's not in.
Boy OK big girl.

*The telegraph boy pushes the telegram through the letterbox and exits.
Sally and Bob Barking enter from the pub*

Bob Oh, come on, Sally!
Sally It's no use, Bob. I've got to give him his chance to be Lord Hareford.
Bob Oh yeah, I get that, but what have you got to leave your own home here
    for?
Sally 'Cos 'e'll only come after me 'ere if I don't. I've written him this letter,
    telling 'im not to look for me, 'cos 'e won't find me. (*She knocks at the
    door*)
Bob Yeah, well it seems all wrong to me.
Sally Bob, if I don't go ...

Mrs Brown comes out of the house with the telegram

Mrs Brown Sally love, there's a telegram come for you. (*She hands Sally
    the telegram*)

Sally For me? I bet it's from Bill. (*She opens and reads the telegram*)
Bob Is it?
Mrs Brown Anything wrong, lovie?
Sally (*handing the telegram to Bob*) What did I tell you?
Bob (*reading*) "Stay put — am giving everything up and coming after you. Love Bill."
Sally Now you see why I've got to go. Goodbye, Bob. Keep your fingers crossed for me.

Sally and Mrs Brown exit into house

Bob (*calling after Sally*) Good luck, Sally.

Bob exits. A Girl enters and passes him

Sir John enters

Girl Hallo, Saucy.
Sir John What an excellent judge of character. (*He looks up and down, lost*)

A Policeman enters

Excuse me, Constable, can you tell me where I can find number twenty-one Capstan Street.
Constable (*in perfect Oxford accent*) For your information, sir, you are already in Capstan Street, even as you ask, and by a further stretch of coincidence, you find yourself immediately outside number twenty-one.
Sir John (*amazed*) Thank you, officer.
Constable Not at all, sir. It gives me great satisfaction to be of any service. That is my function and I perform it with zeal.
Sir John Good lord. Well, thank you. *Dormez bien.*
Constable *Merci bien, monsieur. Bonsoir et les beaux reves.*
Sir John An educated policeman! Whatever next. Ah, here we are. Number twenty-one. (*He knocks at the door*)

Mrs Brown opens the door

Good-evening, madam. Does Miss Sally Smith live here?
Mrs Brown Who wants 'er?
Sir John Say it's her fairy godfather.
Mrs Brown (*taken aback*) Her who?
Sir John Just take me in to her.
Mrs Brown (*barring the way*) Oh no you don't, Not in my house. You filthy beast! (*Calling over her shoulder*) Sally! There's someone to see you.

Sally (*off, calling*) Who is it?
Mrs Brown Says he's your furry godfather.
Sir John Fairy, not furry. It's all right, Sally, it's only me.
Sally (*off*) Coming.

Sally appears on the doorstep

Sir John. What are you doing here?

Mrs Brown is hovering inquisitively

It's all right, Mrs Brown, this is a very dear friend of mine.
Mrs Brown I'm sure. This is what comes of hobnobbing with the gentry.
Sir John Goodbye, fair spirit of morality.

Mrs Brown exits into the house, shutting the door

Now, Sally, what's all this?
Sally It's no good, Sir John, I'm not going back. You're wasting your time.
Sir John I haven't come here to persuade you to go back.
Sally You haven't?
Sir John No. We have to beat the Duchess at her own game.
Sally The Duchess don't like me — I'm not "fit and proper".
Sir John But suppose we made you "fit and proper".
Sally 'Sides, I wouldn't wan' it.
Sir John But there are all sorts of things you could do with a good accent!
    Look at Ronald Coleman or Vivien Leigh.
Sally Well, I've always wanted a little dress shop. (*Suspiciously*) But how
    would you do it?
Sir John Not me — there's an army friend of mine. He shares a house in
    Upper Wimpole Street with a remarkable man who could certainly do it.
    He's done it before. If you love Bill, you'll let him try.
Sally (*after a pause*) All right, I'll come, only if you promise not to tell Bill
    where I am.
Sir John I promise ...
Sally Then can we go now?
Sir John Mmmm ...
Sally Can we go right now, 'cos look. (*She shows him the telegram*) See.
Sir John I'll give me friend a call. I'll be waiting in my car.
Sally I'll run in and pack a few things.
Sir John Good girl. Car's at the end of the street.

Sally opens the door and Mrs Brown falls out. Sally goes in

Mrs Brown Ooh! Oh dear, I've dropped something.
Sir John A couple of eaves, perhaps?
Mrs Brown Well, what if I was listening? It was for Sally's good.
Sir John So, you're Mrs Brown?
Mrs Brown Mrs Anastasia Brown, yes.
Sir John Well, Mrs Anastasia Brown, you evidently heard that I'm going
to take Sally away.
Mrs Brown Yes, I heard that fairy tale you just told the poor girl.
Sir John You flatter me, Mrs Brown. But you also heard that she doesn't
want Bill to know where she's gone. (*He takes out a five pound note*)
Mrs Brown No more you do, I don't suppose.
Sir John (*rustling the note*) Do you know what this is, Mrs Brown?
Mrs Brown It sounds like a fiver.
Sir John Does it look like a fiver?
Mrs Brown It is a fiver.
Sir John (*handing the note to her*) Here you are then — (*he snatches away
the fiver*) — if you keep your mouth shut when Bill comes for her.
Mrs Brown I get you, sir, Mum's the word.
Sir John Good. Tell Sally I'll be waiting in the car. Farewell, Mrs Anastasia
Brown.

The Girl approaches Sir John

Not now. This is war, and I must rejoin my regiment.

Sir John exits. Bill enters

Bill Oi! Oi! I recognize that face!
Mrs Brown Oh my gawd! I mean, oh, my Lord.
Bill Don't you start, Mrs B. Where's Sally. (*He shouts*) Oi! Sal! Sal!
Mrs Brown She's gone. Not here. Gone.
Bill Gone? Whatcher mean, gone?
Mrs Brown She didn't say. She went away. Not coming back no more.
Bill When?
Mrs Brown When? Ooh, ages ago.
Bill 'Ere, did she get my wire then?
Mrs Brown Yes-no ... I mean, yes, that's what made her go.
Bill She leave an address?
Mrs Brown No address.
Bill What about her mail?
Mrs Brown Well, she'll collect it, I mean, I don't know.
Bill You telling me pork pies, Mrs B? She in there?
Mrs Brown No! She ain't! She's gone, I tell you!

Bill Oh yeah. I've heard that before. I'll wait 'ere.

Mrs Brown It's no good, Bill, she'll never come back.

Bill Oh, won't she? We'll soon see about that. (*He leans against the lamppost*)

Mrs Brown goes indoors. The policeman re-enters

Constable Now then, sir, I'm terribly afraid that you really can't stop here. It rather comes under the heading of loitering. Are you waiting for someone?

Music 20: Leaning on a Lamppost

Bill
Leaning on a lamp
Maybe you think I look a tramp
Or you may think I'm hanging round to steal a car
But no I'm not a crook
And if you think that's what I look
I'll tell you why I'm here and what my motives are

I'm leaning on a lamppost
At the corner of the street
In case a certain little lady comes by
Oh me, oh my, I hope the little lady comes by

I don't know if she'll get away
She doesn't always get away
But any way I know that she'll try
Oh, me, oh my, I hope the little lady comes by.

There's no other girl I could wait for
But this one I'd break any date for
I won't have to ask what she's late for
She wouldn't leave me flat
She's not a girl like that
She's absolutely wonderful
And marvellous and beautiful
And anyone can understand why ——

I'm leaning on a lamppost
At the corner of the street
In case a certain little lady comes by

Dance — The Lamppost Ballet

The dancers enter

Bill searches for Sally. He returns to the lamppost as they dance. They freeze as Sally enters in a cloud of dry ice and dances with Bill. Sally exits and the dancers come to life again

> There's no other girl I could wait for
> But this one I'd break any date for
> I won't have to ask what she's late for
> She wouldn't leave me flat
> She's not a girl like that
> She's absolutely wonderful
> And marvellous and beautiful
> And anyone can understand why ——
>
> I'm leaning on a lamppost
> At the corner of the street
> In case a certain little lady comes by

The dancers exit leaving Bill alone leaning on the lamppost

Sally watches from the upstairs window

Mrs Brown comes out of the house and hands Bill a note. Bill crumples the note and tosses it into the dustbin; Mrs Brown tries to console him

Music 20A: Leaning on a Lamppost: Tag

> I'm leaning on a lamppost
> At the corner of the street
> In case a certain little lady comes by

Bill blows out the lamp and the Lights fade to Black-out

SCENE 4

Hareford Hall

The Lights come up

Music 21: The Hunt Ball

The Hunt Ball is in progress. Jaquie, Gerald and the guests, in hunting dress pink, are dancing a gallop

Bill enters through the front doors and gives Charles his coat. Jaquie attempts to latch on to Bill, but the dancers lead off, and Gerald pulls her away

Bill exits disconsolately

Sir John enters and watches the end of the dance from the stairs as the dancers exit leaving Sir Jasper

The Duchess enters with the Battersbys and Parchester, who continue out on to the terrace, leaving the Duchess and Sir John together

Sir John How now, Maria. You've been moping for days. What's the matter, bad news from your bookmaker?

Duchess Oh, John, I just despair of William. Since Sal went away he has become impossible. He's wasted thousands on detectives to look for her, newspaper advertisements, offering huge rewards. Nothing. And he's convinced that I know where she is. I could almost wish the wretched girl back here.

Sir John Ah, well, you never know. Perhaps she will come back. Stranger things have happened.

Duchess It's so dispiriting.

Sir John Well, Maria, I never thought I'd say it, but I preferred you when you were a ghastly old trout. Do cheer up.

Duchess Usually I buy myself a new hat if I'm down in the dumps.

Sir John So that's where you get them from.

Duchess I never realized how truly fond of her William is. I thought when she was out of the way ... but he's done nothing but sulk.

Sir John I know, he's just not the same, is he? (*He shows the Duchess his gold watch*) But, it's never too late. I knew a couple once who had secretly loved each other for thirty years

Duchess Thirty years?

Sir John Thirty-one years, seven months and three days. Their love was so secret that they weren't even aware of it themselves.

Duchess And what happened?

Sir John Well, they struggled miserably along ... until one day the man took it into his head ... after all this time, to get down on one knee, not unlike this, (*he demonstrates*) and say in his simple, direct, manly way, "I can't move".

Duchess I can't move?
Sir John Dammit, Maria, my leg's seized up. Hit my back.

The Duchess complies

Higher. Left a bit. Harder. That's it.
Duchess Oh, John.
Sir John Damned shrapnel. Always gives a twinge when I get worked up. Where was I?
Duchess This couple. The man was about to propose.
Sir John Oh, Maria. (*He bends to kiss her*)

Charles enters

Duchess Oh, John.

Charles clears his throat. The Duchess points to Charles, but Sir John, thinking they are still alone, takes the gesture as an indication that they should go upstairs to be alone. He points to the balcony

Sir John Oh, yes.
Duchess Oh, no.

The Duchess exits. Charles coughs again

Good heavens, Charles, you here?
Charles Yes, sir.
Sir John Women, Charles.
Charles Yes, sir.
Sir John Have you ever been in love, Charles?
Charles Oh, no, sir. I'm married.
Sir John Really? I had no idea.
Charles To the cook, sir. You were kind enough to attend the sentence ... er, ceremony.
Sir John Was I? Be that as it may: is she here yet?
Charles Yes, sir, she's just arrived, sir.
Sir John You put her where I told you to?
Charles Yes, sir.
Sir John Good man. And remember, not a word to anyone, and wait for my signal.

Parchester enters

Parchester Everything going according to plan, Sir John?

Jaquie and Gerald enter

Sir John (*to Parchester*) Quiet, Cyril ... Cecil ... Cedric!

Sir John and Parchester exit

Jaquie Charles.
Charles My Lady?
Jaquie Have you see Lord Hareford?
Charles I believe he is in his bedroom, Lady Jaqueline.
Jaquie Bedroom, at this time of the day? What's he doing?
Charles I believe he's packing, my Lady.
Jaquie Packing? What on earth is he packing for?
Charles He did not confide in me, my Lady.
Gerald I told you so.
Jaquie Charles.
Charles My Lady.
Jaquie Ask Lord Hareford to come here, please.
Charles Very good, my Lady.

Charles exits

Gerald Well, frankly Jaquie, you're making a complete ass of yourself. Chasing after Bill Hareford when you know he's done nothing but search for Sally! Just give up this nonsense and marry me!
Jaquie Marry you? With all your debts? Ha!
Gerald (*chasing Jaquie upstage on his knees*) As a matter of fact I don't have any debts. Bill was good enough to write me a big cheque.

Bill enters

Bill Olly! Olly! Olly! All fresh! Ripe strawberries! You rang, madam?
Jaquie Oh, William.

Bill throws his hat off stage

The Duchess enters with Bill's hat on her head

Duchess What is the meaning of this?
Jaquie Oh, Mummy! Oh, William, you're not really packing to go.
Bill And what's more, I am leaving, unless the Duchess produces Sally.
Duchess How many times do I have to tell you ——
Jaquie Sally! Sally! And what about me! I'm not to be cast aside lightly.
Bill No, you should be thrown with great force.
Jaquie But don't you feel something when we're together?
Bill Ill.

Jaquie But I thought you cared for me.
Bill I couldn't care for you. I'm just an ordinary Earl, not a vet.
Jaquie Let me tell you, I wouldn't marry you now if you were the last man on earth.
Bill If I were the last man on earth I'd be too busy to marry anybody.
Jaquie (*slapping Bill's face*) Oh!

Jaquie exits

Gerald I say, that was a slap in the face. It would have served her right if you'd slapped her in the face.
Bill It's not her face wants slapping.
Gerald Yes, but you couldn't very well ...
Bill No, but she'd marry the first man who does.
Gerald She would? I say do you really think so? I'd never thought of that. Tally Ho!

Gerald exits with determination

Duchess William, where are you planning to go?
Bill Lambeth, Aunty.
Duchess Oh, but this is madness, madness.

There is the sound of a slap, off

Jaquie (*off*) Ooh!
Duchess Haven't I done enough for you, haven't I thrown parties for you?
Bill At me.
Duchess You must have a son to ensure the succession, or better still lots of sons.
Bill You've got a mind like a rabbit.
Duchess There are dozens of girls falling over themselves to become your wife.

There is the sound of another slap, off

Jaquie (*off*) Ooh!
Bill Lord Hareford's wife. Only one girl ever wanted to be my wife.
Duchess You can't go now, William, not after all I've achieved.
Bill I can unless you tell me where Sally is.
Duchess I don't know where she is.

There is the sound of another slap, off

Jaquie (*off*) Ooh, Gerald!
Bill Then tomorrow every picture palace in London'll show a newsreel of
Lord Hareford going back to Lambeth.

Gerald and Jaquie enter. Jaquie is rather flushed

Gerald I say, I say, you'll never guess what's happened. Jaqueline has
promised to be my trouble and strife.
Bill Aaah! Gerald, sorry. And now I'm going back to Lambeth to make Sally
be my wife.
Duchess And make the same mistake as your father.
Bill The only mistake he made was to leave his girl. I shan't. I'm sorry Aunty
Duchess, you seem to have lost your little battle.
Duchess I hope I'm not ungracious in defeat. You may kiss your aunt.
Bill No, you may kiss your nevvie.
Duchess I will. (*She kisses his cheek*) Goodbye, Bill. You're a true Hareford.
Bill And so are you. Right! Cheerie-bye everyone! I'm off to finish packing.

Bill exits

Sir John Gerald, go and fetch him back, quick.
Gerald What for?
Sir John You'll see.

Gerald exits

Sir John takes Sir Jasper's ear trumpet and blows it like a hunting horn

The family, guests and Charles enter

Charles Miss Sally Smith.
Duchess Who?
Jaquie What?

Music 22: Sally's Entrance

Sally enters, superbly dressed and carrying a fan

Sally (*curtsying to the Duchess*) Your Grace. Lady Jaqueline. Gentlemen.
(*She waves*)
Duchess What does this mean?
Sally (*looking at Sir John*) We're all of us susceptible to the right treatment,
your Grace.
Sir John I think she's got it.

Duchess You, John?

Sir John inclines his head

John, you ... Oh, my goodness, Sally. Does Bill know?
Sally Not yet.

Gerald enters

Gerald He's on his way.

Bill enters with two suitcases, which he puts down in front of the Duchess and Jaquie

Sally covers her face with the fan

Sir John William, my boy. I would like you to meet a special young friend of mine.
Sally (*hiding her face with her fan*) How do you do, Lord Hareford.
Bill How do you do? Can you get the car round please, Charles?
Sally Do I take it that you are going somewhere, Lord Hareford? What are those two bags doing? (*She points at the cases in front of the Duchess and Jaquie*)
Bill They live here. Right, I'm packed and I'm off.
Sally Back to Lambeth I understand.
Bill That's right, yeah. To find Sally.
Sally It seems to me, Lord Hareford, and you'll forgive me for saying so, that you must be extremely fond of this girl to give everything up for her like this.
Bill If you only knew how much I wanted her to come back.
Sally And if she comes back, Lord Hareford, what on earth will you say to her after all this time?
Bill What'll I say? What'll I say? — I'll tell you what I'd say.

Sally lowers her fan

(*Seeing Sally*) Where the bloody hell have you been?

CURTAIN

Finale

Music 23: Love Makes the World Go Round (Reprise)

Chorus   Without love nobody would sing
                Without love no wedding bells ring
                The world keeps on turning

                You can't stop it turning
                For love makes the world go round

                An old love, a new love
                So long as it's true love

                It's love makes the world go round
                Without love nobody would sing
                Without love no wedding bells ring
                And though people doubt it
                They can't live without it
                All over the world they've found
                That love makes the world go round

Me And My Girl (Reprise)

Bill   ⎫   Me and my girl, meant for each other
Sir John   ⎬   Sent for each other, and liking it so
Gerald   ⎭   Me and my girl, 's' no use pretending
                    We knew the ending a long time ago

Sally   ⎫   Some little church, with a big steeple
Duchess   ⎪   Just a few people that both of us know
Jaquie   ⎬   And we'll have love ——
Chorus   ⎭

All   —— laughter
                Be happy ever after, me and my girl

Curtain Calls

Music 24: The Lambeth Walk (Reprise)

                Any time you're Lambeth way
                Any evening, any day

You'll find us all
Doing the Lambeth Walk

Every little Lambeth gal
With her little Lambeth pal
You'll find them all
Doing the Lambeth Walk. Oi!

Everything free and easy
So do as you darn well pleasey
Why don't you make your way there?
Go there, stay there

Once you get down Lambeth way
Every evening, every day
You'll find yourself
Doing the Lambeth
Doing the Lambeth Walk

Music 25: Leaning On A Lamppost (Reprise)

All

I'm leaning on a lamppost
At the corner of the street
In case a certain little lady comes by
Oh me, oh my, I hope the little lady comes by

I don't know if she'll get away
She doesn't always get away
But anyway I know that she'll try
Oh me, oh my, I hope the little lady comes by

There's no other girl I could wait for
But this one I'd break any date for
I won't have to ask what she's late for
She wouldn't leave me flat
She's not a girl like that

She's absolutely wonderful
And marvellous and beautiful
And anyone can understand why ——

I'm leaning on a lamppost
At the corner of the street
In case a certain little lady comes by

Music 26: The Lambeth Walk (Reprise)

All   Any time you're Lambeth way
                         Any evening, any day
                         You'll find us all
                         Doing the Lambeth Walk

                         Every little Lambeth gal
                         With her little Lambeth pal
                         You'll find them all
                         Doing the Lambeth Walk — Oi!

                         Everything free and easy
                         So do as you darn well pleasey
                         Why don't you make your way there?
                         Go there, stay there

                         Once you get down Lambeth way
                         Every evening, every day
                         You'll find yourself
                         Doing the Lambeth
                         Doing the Lambeth Walk

FURNITURE AND PROPERTY LIST

ACT I
SCENE 1

On stage: MAYFAIR
Items of luggage making up car for **Guests**

INTERIOR OF HAREFORD HALL
Suit of armour
Two long tables set for grand buffet
Dining chairs
Occasional table. *On it:* vase of flowers, letter rack, newspaper
Plates
Glasses
Whisky and brandy decanters

Personal: **Jaquie**: Engagement ring
Bill: Cigarette, pack of cards
Sir John: Gold pocket watch
Sir Jasper: Ear trumpet (used throughout)

SCENE 2

Strike: All the above except buffet tables; just remove food and cloths from them

Set: Pots and pans
General kitchen paraphernalia
Plate for **Parlour Maid**
Glass of beer for **Charles**
Saucepan and spoon for **Cook**

SCENE 3

Strike: All the above except one table

Re-set: Table to L as a desk

Set: Small chesterfield with cushions
On desk: letters, bell

Off stage:	Cricket bat (**Gerald**)
	Cricket pads, cap, bat for **Bill** (**Dancers**)
	Riding mac (**Charles**)
	Hunting jacket, deerstalker, shotgun (**Footman**)

| *Personal*: | **Bill**: Sir John's watch |

On cue p. 30

| *Strike*: | Chesterfield |
| | Desk |

Set:	Upright piano
	Bar
	Bar stools
	Tables
	Glasses of beer (**Farmers, Locals**)

SCENE 4

No additional props

SCENE 5

| *Strike*: | All the above |

| *Set*: | Table |

| *Off stage*: | Cutlery, crockery, glasses etc. (**Servants**) |
| | Trays of glasses of sherry (**Servants**) |

| *Personal*: | **Bill**: Straw |
| | **Cockneys**: Spoons |

ACT II

SCENE 1

On stage:	Croquet mallets, hoops and balls
	Tea things
	Trays of drinks

| *Off stage*: | Suitcase (**Sally**) |

During song p.47

Strike: All the above

Set: Bookcase. *On it*: classical bust
                 Small drinks table
                 Large round table. *On it*: ancient tomes, decanter, glasses, napkins
                 Mobile library steps
                 Tiger-skin rug
                 Chairs
                 Huge ancient volume for **Bill** containing cut-out tree

SCENE 2

Strike: All the above

Off stage: Cup hilt rapier (**Bill**)
                 Tea trolley (**Parlour Maid**)

Personal: **Parchester**: Pocket watch
                 Bill: **Sir John**'s watch

SCENE 3

Strike: All the above

Set: Dustbin

Off stage: Bicycle, telegram (**Telegraph Boy**)
                 Note (**Mrs Brown**)

Personal: **Sir John**: Five pound note

SCENE 4

Strike: Dustbin

Set: As HAREFORD HALL section of ACT I SCENE 1

Off stage: Two suitcases (**Bill**)

Personal: **Sally**: fan

LIGHTING PLOT

Practical fittings required: lamppost
Various settings: three exteriors, five interiors

ACT I, SCENE 1

To open:	General exterior lighting	
Cue 1	House revolves *General interior lighting*	(Page 3)
Cue 2	**Bill**: "I've got enough to carry as it is." *Fade lights*	(Page 18)

ACT I, SCENE 2

To open:	General interior lighting	
Cue 3	**Servants**: " ... an English gentleman." *Fade lights*	(Page 21)

ACT I, SCENE 3

To open:	General interior lighting	
Cue 4	**Servants** exit *Cross-fade to Hareford Arms lighting*	(Page 31)

ACT I, SCENE 4

Cue 5	**Sally**: "You've got to follow your heart." *Fade lights*	(Page 33)

ACT I, SCENE 5

To open:	General exterior lighting

No cues

ACT II, Scene 1

To open: General exterior lighting

Cue 6   **Sally**: "And smile, smile, smile!"   (Page 48)
             Fade lights

ACT II, Scene 2

To open: General interior lighting

Cue 7   **Bill** produces **Sir John**'s watch   (Page 60)
             Fade lights

ACT II, Scene 3

To open: General exterior lighting

Cue 8   **Bill** blows out lamp   (Page 65)
             Fade lights to black-out

ACT II, Scene 4

To open: General exterior lighting

             No cues

Finale

To open: As ACT II, Scene 4

EFFECTS PLOT

ACT I